PRAISE FOR *LINCOLN'S GIFT*

"In this compact, user-friendly volume, Gordon Leidner ingeniously blends a study of Lincoln's humor with an account of his life, showing how our sixteenth president was not always a 'man of sorrows' but often a man of laughter, capable alike of enjoying as well as telling a good story."

—Michael Burlingame, Chancellor Naomi B. Lynn Distinguished Chair in Lincoln studies, University of Illinois at Springfield, and author of *Abraham Lincoln: A Life*

"A sense of humor was one of Lincoln's greatest gifts. His contemporaries recognized it, and we still benefit from it today. Gordon Leidner has brought together a compact history of Lincoln's life, peppered with wonderful anecdotes and stories that reflect the best of Lincoln's wit."

—Jonathan W. White, PhD, assistant professor of American studies, Christopher Newport University, and author of *Lincoln on Law, Leadership, and Life*

"Gordon Leidner's *Lincoln's Gift* is simply the best book that has been published on this great president's humor and stories. Skillfully placed in the context of Lincoln's life and career, the book demonstrates Lincoln's phenomenal ability to recall stories or make a quip for almost any occasion in order to make a point or to entertain listeners. His stories also served as a form of catharsis for his own melancholy. As Leidner shows, most of Lincoln's anecdotes were drawn from his rural Midwestern background and, as Lincoln admitted, many were not all original with him. Everyone interested in Abraham Lincoln will want to read this book and also have a copy of it on their desk for reference and for family and friends."

—William C. Harris, emeritus professor of
history, North Carolina State University, and
author of *Lincoln and the Border States*

"Gordon Leidner provides a pleasant, readable narrative of Lincoln's life and times. His reliance on Lincoln's humorous quotes and metaphors opens windows to view Lincoln's humanity, humor, and remarkable sensitivity."

—Charles M. Hubbard, PhD, professor of history and
Lincoln historian, Lincoln Memorial University

LINCOLN'S GIFT

HOW HUMOR SHAPED LINCOLN'S LIFE & LEGACY

GORDON LEIDNER

with an afterword by Michael Burlingame

CUMBERLAND HOUSE™

Published by Cumberland House, an imprint of Sourcebooks, Inc.
P.O. Box 4410, Naperville, Illinois 60567-4410
(630) 961-3900
Fax: (630) 961-2168
www.sourcebooks.com

Library of Congress Cataloging-in-Publication Data

Leidner, Gordon
  Lincoln's gift : how humor shaped Lincoln's life and legacy / Gordon Leidner.
     pages cm
  Includes bibliographical references and index.
  (hard cover : alk. paper) 1. Lincoln, Abraham, 1809–1865—Humor. 2. Lincoln, Abraham, 1809–1865—Anecdotes. 3. American wit and humor. I. Title.
  E457.2.L45 2015
  973.7092—dc23

                                      2014041682

                Printed and bound in the United States of America.
                     WOZ 10 9 8 7 6 5 4 3 2 1

In memory of my brother:

Jeffrey David Leidner

Who walked on straight paths.

CONTENTS

INTRODUCTION
LINCOLN THE STORYTELLER

They say I tell a great many stories; I reckon I do, but I have found in the course of a long experience that common people, take them as they run, are more easily informed through the medium of broad illustration than in any other way, and as to what the hypercritical few may think, I don't care.

—Abraham Lincoln

Today we think of Abraham Lincoln as a great leader—perhaps our greatest. We recall his eloquent speeches, his fight for the preservation of the Union, and his emancipation of the slaves. We honor his devotion to duty, sacrifice, and honesty.

What we do not think of today in association with Abraham Lincoln is a good joke. In Lincoln's day, however, he was a well-known storyteller, and more than one Lincoln joke book was published during his presidency. Although most of the jokes in them did not originate with

Lincoln, like everyone else, he enjoyed reading them. One of them had a story Lincoln was particularly fond of—the anecdote about two Quaker women discussing President Lincoln and Confederate president Jefferson Davis at the beginning of the Civil War. The first Quaker lady said, after some contemplation, that she believed the Confederacy would win the war because "Jefferson Davis is a praying man." "But Abraham Lincoln is a praying man too," the second Quaker lady protested. "Yes," the first admitted, "but the Lord will think Abraham is joking."

Mark Twain said that the secret source of humor is not joy but sorrow, and if this is true, we can understand why Lincoln told so many jokes. He endured many tragedies in his life, beginning with the loss of his mother when he was nine years old, his sister when he was nineteen, his first love when in his twenties, two young sons, and of course the terrible trials of an internecine war.

Lincoln always said that he cared little for the typical vices of the day—drinking, smoking, or gambling—but that a good joke was like a tonic or medicine to him. It is well known that Lincoln had a melancholy personality and frequently suffered bouts of what may have been unipolar depression. He recognized this challenge and told many people that he used funny stories to help lift himself out of sessions of sadness.[1]

Lincoln acquired his penchant for jokes and storytelling from his father,

---

1. A thorough analysis of Lincoln's melancholy can be found in Shenk, *Lincoln's Melancholy.*

Thomas Lincoln. When Abe was a child, he loved to listen to his father and other men swap yarns and funny stories. As he grew older, he himself became increasingly adept at telling and retelling humorous stories, frequently modifying them to accommodate each situation. When Lincoln became a lawyer, he used his jokes and stories to gain the good will of juries, and more than once, the opposing counsel complained to the judge that Lincoln's stories were irrelevant and distracting. The trouble for them, though, was that the portly Eighth Circuit judge, David Davis, loved Lincoln's jokes more than anyone else in the courtroom.

As a politician, Lincoln used his humorous stories to ridicule opponents, such as the competing political party whose platform he said was like "the pair of pantaloons" advertised to be "large enough for any man, small enough for any boy." More than once, Lincoln's lifelong political opponent, Democrat Stephen A. Douglas, saw his forceful arguments forgotten by the audience when Lincoln followed up his rival's speech with a joke or funny analogy. At the debate in Ottawa, Illinois, Lincoln compared one of Douglas's statements to trying to make a chestnut horse into a horse chestnut. At the debate in Alton, Lincoln told a story that showed how he felt about a political feud that was currently raging between Douglas and the head of the Democratic Party, President James Buchanan. He said he felt like the old woman who, not knowing who was going to win a brawl between her husband and a bear, decided to cheer for both of them: "Go it husband, go it bear!"

When Lincoln became president, he used his jokes for various purposes. Sometimes his jokes put visitors at ease, such as the time he met a soldier who was three inches taller than him, and he asked the young man if he knew "when his feet get cold." Sometimes his jokes were just for fun, like when he commented about the demise of a vain general, saying, "if he had known how big his funeral would be, he would have died long ago." Often his jokes were simply familiar expressions, as with his comment to a sculptor who had been working on a bust of Lincoln, when he said "that looks very much like the critter," or to a visitor that he would "pitch in" to his problem "like a dog at a root."

Frequently Lincoln used jokes to illustrate political points he wanted to make, such as his comparison of General George B. McClellan's continuous cry for reinforcements to the monkey named Jocko who wanted a longer tail. On another occasion, he compared the congressman who was taking both sides of a political issue to the farmer and son who had to search both sides of a branch at the same time for their old sow who they thought "was on both sides of the creek." Sometimes he used jokes to get visitors who had taken up too much of his time to leave. While the listeners were laughing, he would ease them out the door.

Lincoln also used funny stories to break the ice in awkward moments. Frequently these jokes were simple ones that poked fun at his own appearance, like the story of meeting a stranger in a railroad car in Illinois. The stranger said, "Excuse me, Sir, but I have an article in my possession which belongs to you."

"How is that?" Lincoln asked, considerably astonished.

The stranger took a jackknife from his pocket. "This knife," he said, "was placed in my hands some years ago, with the injunction that I was to keep it until I found a man uglier than myself. I have carried it from that time to this. Allow me now to say, Sir, that I think you are fairly entitled to the property."

More than anything else, however, Lincoln used humor to help him cope with his melancholia and the terrible strain he had during the war. He told one visitor that if he didn't tell these stories, "he would die."

It is not the intention of *Lincoln's Gift* to be a joke book but instead a short biography that weaves many of his jokes and humorous stories into the narrative. The jokes and funny stories included herein are placed, as accurately as possible, within the context that Lincoln actually used them, or when this is not known, when he would likely have used them.

A challenge for anyone who wants to recount a funny Lincoln story is to select the genuine article. Spurious Lincoln jokes abound, and even for Lincoln scholars, it can sometimes be difficult to discern which stories Lincoln actually told. To minimize this problem, I have taken the jokes and stories from the sources in the bibliography and cross-checked them, where possible, with the appropriate primary sources listed at the end of the book.

Another challenge is to place the jokes correctly in the timeline of Lincoln's life. Although most can be accurately placed chronologically, some are more difficult. For some stories, there are varying or insufficient accounts of when Lincoln told them. Also, he often repeated stories throughout his life, with slight variations to meet each circumstance.

The biggest challenge, however, in conveying Lincoln's humor is that his skill as a storyteller and his manner of delivery were often funnier than the story itself. As the great Lincoln biographer Benjamin Thomas pointed out, Lincoln's facial expressions, gestures, Hoosier accent, and his ability to mimic were essential to getting a laugh from his audience.[2] Although this cannot be adequately conveyed in print, in an effort to remind the reader of Lincoln's manner of speech, Lincoln's Hoosier accent has been preserved, as much as possible, in quoted material. In a few instances, stories were abbreviated or altered slightly for clarity.

Abraham Lincoln the statesman definitely deserves the credit he's received for his great accomplishments—leading America through its most terrible war, preserving the Union, inspiring the nation to sacrifice, and freeing the slaves. But to fully appreciate Lincoln's accomplishments, one must understand how he coped with the war casualties, his personal tragedies, and his melancholia. To do this, we take a brief look at Abraham Lincoln, from his lighter side.

Gordon Leidner
September 1, 2014

---

2. For an analysis of Lincoln's humor, see Thomas, "Lincoln's Humor: An Analysis," chap. 1 in *"Lincoln's Humor" and Other Essays.*

NEVER COME TO MUCH
1809-1830

Abraham Lincoln was born on February 12, 1809, in a log cabin near the village of Hodgenville, Kentucky. Most of the world didn't take notice of this event, but when Abraham's nine-year-old cousin Dennis Hanks heard of it, he followed a custom in Kentucky to "run over and greet the newborn babe." Abraham's mother, Nancy, was glad to see Dennis, and wanting to see the young man squirm, she shoved the baby into his arms.

Dennis held little Abraham dutifully and looked him over from head to toe. Before long, the future president of the United States began to cry, and nothing Dennis could do would stop the squawking. Finally Dennis had endured enough and handed his red-faced little cousin back to his mother, saying disgustedly, "Take him—he'll never come to much."

Dennis's assessment of young Abraham's prospects was not an unreasonable one, considering the circumstances of his birth. He was from a poor family, lived in an area of the country that offered little opportunity for education, and seemed destined for a life of hardscrabble farm work.

In spite of his challenges, Abraham had been given the advantages of a loving mother, a hardworking father, and good health. In addition to these, he had a pleasant disposition and even as a youth would become well liked by both children and adults. But most significantly, he possessed a tremendous hunger to learn, an extraordinary memory, and a lifelong desire to be "esteemed of my fellow men."

According to Cousin Dennis, Nancy Lincoln was an intelligent woman who was quite influential in her children's intellectual development. Abraham's father, Thomas Lincoln, cared little for education but was a likable character with a unique talent for composing and telling humorous stories.

Thomas was a carpenter and cabinetmaker by trade, and like nearly everyone else in that region, he was a farmer as well. When Abraham was two years old, Thomas moved Abraham, Nancy, and Abraham's four-year-old sister Sarah from Sinking Spring Farm to a more fertile farm along Knob Creek. The Lincolns lived at the Knob Creek farm for five years, and while there, Nancy gave birth to another boy, named Thomas after his father, who unfortunately died in infancy.

By most accounts, Thomas and Nancy Lincoln were honest people who were respected members of their community as well as of the Little Mount Separate Baptist Church. Nancy was deeply religious and took pleasure in reading the Bible to the children. Reading books would become a passion for Abraham Lincoln, and the Bible was the first book that, through the voice of his mother, would open his eyes to a larger world. According to Dennis, Nancy "learned him to read the Bible" and Abraham was "much moved by the stories."

Although Nancy could read and put great stock in her children's education, her husband could not and did not. Of above average height and powerful build, Thomas valued hard work, as evidenced by the fact he had saved enough money to buy the Knob Creek farm. Dennis recalled that Thomas was very popular in the community, because he was "a good, clean, social, truthful, & honest man, loving like his wife everything and everybody."

Although in the evenings Thomas liked to entertain his family with stories about Daniel Boone, a distant relative, and other pioneers of Kentucky, life at Knob Creek was primarily about survival. On the farm, the children had many chores to do, and so Abraham and Sarah had little opportunity for formal education. In Kentucky, they attended local ABC schools for at least two brief sessions, one taught by a hardy soul named Zachariah Riney, and the other by a large man who was related to Nancy by marriage, Caleb Hazel. These "masters" were employed as much for their ability to maintain discipline as their ability to instruct their pupils.

In December 1816, Abraham's father uprooted the family again, this time moving north of the Ohio River into the recently developed state of

Indiana. Unlike Kentucky, Indiana was a free state. Although he disliked slavery, Thomas's primary reason for moving was probably to get away from Kentucky, where he frequently ran afoul of property title disputes resulting from poorly conducted state land surveys.

Thomas moved his family to a virtual wilderness, a heavily wooded area close to the Ohio River. Along Little Pigeon Creek, near Gentryville, he built a crude shelter of logs enclosed on only three sides, with the fourth side facing an open fire. Somehow, the family survived the winter of 1816–17 in this hovel.

In Indiana, Thomas owned eighty acres of land with undisputed title. When the spring of 1817 arrived, eight-year-old Abraham had an ax put in his hand for the purpose of helping his father clear their land and build a better cabin. That fall, Nancy's uncle and aunt, Thomas and Elizabeth Sparrow, arrived and brought with them Dennis, who was now eighteen years old.

Although the family's situation improved from the previous winter, the fall of 1818 brought heartache. Both Thomas and Elizabeth Sparrow came down with a deadly ailment known as "milk sickness." Contracted from the milk of cows that had eaten a poisonous plant known as snakeroot, the sickness almost always resulted in a quick death. Doctors were scarce in that part of the country, and within a week, both Thomas and Elizabeth Sparrow were dead. The Lincolns had very little time to grieve, because soon Abraham's mother Nancy contracted milk sickness too.

Nancy quickly grew weak and realized that she was going to die. She called Abraham and Sarah to her bedside, told them she was not going to live, and encouraged them to be "good and kind to their father, to one another, and to the world." She also expressed hope that they would "reverence and worship God." Within hours, she was gone. Her grieving husband and son built a simple wooden coffin from whipsawed pine logs, and they buried her near their cabin.

Dennis moved in with the Lincoln family and shared the loft with Abraham. Life became very difficult for the survivors, especially eleven-year-old Sarah, who tried to cook and keep up with household chores. Thomas and Dennis hunted, and Abe did other chores, but Thomas knew that his children needed a mother. In December 1819, he left the family and went to Kentucky to find a wife.

Thomas was a fast mover, for in a few weeks he returned with his new wife, widow Sarah Bush Johnston, her three children, and a wagon-full of much-needed furniture and household furnishings. One can only imagine what the new bride thought of the place she was to call home. The roof was half-finished, the door was broken, there were no windows, and there was no cabin floor. The children were not very impressive either. Abe and Sarah looked "wild—ragged and dirty."

Thomas's new wife, who he called Sally, took charge of the children and home. She immediately soaped and scrubbed Abe and Sarah and dressed them in clothes she'd brought along, making them look "more human."

She put Thomas and Dennis to work fixing up the cabin. They completed the roof, put in windows and a better door, and installed a wooden floor.[1]

Sally was a kindhearted, loving person who took an immediate interest in Abraham and Sarah. In later years, she would say, "Abe was the best boy I ever saw or ever expect to see." Although he would come to dislike being called Abe, he evidently didn't mind hearing this moniker come from his stepmother's lips. Abe affectionately called her Mama.

Life became more pleasant for Abe. He not only had a sister, but now he had the three Johnston children and Dennis to pal around with.

At the age of ten or eleven, Abe attended a term of "blab" school, where students recited lessons aloud at the same time so the master knew they were studying. The school building was a log cabin, located about two miles from the Lincoln home. The schoolmaster was Andrew Crawford, who tried to teach "manners" but focused mostly on reading, writing, and arithmetic through simple proportions.

A term of school at that time was two or three months in length, usually during the winter months when the children were not involved in planting or harvesting crops. It was at Crawford's school that, according to his classmate Nathaniel Grigsby, Abe wrote short essays against cruelty to animals. Crawford, as was typical of schoolteachers in the wilderness, was not especially qualified to teach but was presumably smarter than his students.

---

1. For Sarah Johnston's impact on the Lincoln household, see Burlingame, *Abraham Lincoln: A Life*, 1:27.

Educated people were uncommon in that region, and as an adult, Lincoln would recall that "there were some schools, so called; but no qualification was ever required of a teacher, beyond 'readin, writin, and cipherin,' to the Rule of Three. If a straggler supposed to understand latin, happened to so-journ in the neighborhood, he was looked upon as a wizzard."

Schoolmaster Crawford held spelling contests regularly, and at one of them, Abe helped out fellow student Anna Roby when she was given the word "defied" to spell. She started off correctly with *d-e-f*, then paused, unsure if the next letter was *y* or *i*. She looked at Abe, who was pointing to his eye, and finished the word correctly.

One of the most humorous incidents of Lincoln's school years was a story he would later use, as president, to refer to three cantankerous congressmen. In school, it was customary for students to take turns reading out loud from the Bible. On one occasion, the class read the story of Nebuchadnezzar and the Golden Image from the third chapter of Daniel. Verse 12, which contains the names Shadrach, Meshach, and Abednego, the Israelites who were

Abraham Lincoln's father, Thomas Lincoln

thrown into the fiery furnace, fell to an undersized boy called Bud, whose reading skills had not progressed very far. These names are repeated throughout the chapter. In recounting his recollections of Bud's ordeal, Lincoln said:

> Little Bud stumbled on Shadrach, floundered on Meshach, and went all to pieces on Abednego. Instantly the hand of the master dealt him a cuff on the side of the head and left him wailing and blubbering as the next boy in line took up the reading. But before the girl at the end of the line had done reading he had subsided into sniffles and finally became quiet. His blunder and disgrace were forgotten by the others of the class until his turn was approaching to read again. Then, like a thunderclap out of a clear sky, he sent up a wail which even alarmed the master, who with rather unusual gentleness inquired, "What's the matter now?"

Pointing with a shaking finger at the verse that a few moments later would fall to him to read, Bud managed to quaver out an answer:

> "Look there, marster," he cried, "there comes them same damn three fellers again!"

At Crawford's blab school, Abe and his sister used a textbook they had brought with them from Kentucky, an edition of *Dilworth's Spelling Book*. Through this book, they learned about Roman and Arabic numerals and letters. Many of the lessons were taken from the Psalms and Proverbs of the Bible, and it included the familiar children's prayer, "Now I lay me down to sleep…"

Abe's stepmother recalled that Abe "read all the books he could get his hands on." These included *The Arabian Nights*, *Aesop's Fables*, *Pilgrim's Progress*, Mason Weems's *Life of Washington*, schoolbooks such as *The Kentucky Preceptor*, and, of course, the Bible.

As a farmer's son, Abe couldn't spend a lot of time reading. One of Abe's routine chores as a youth was to go to the local grain mill to grind corn. On one occasion, after arriving at the mill, he hooked up their old mare to the arm of the corn grinder and began urging her along. Having previously complained that "his dog could eat the meal as fast as the horse could grind it," he decided that to speed the mare up, he would occasionally prod her with "Get up, you old hussy!" and apply a switch. The mare evidently grew tired of this routine. In the midst of Abe's admonishment, after he said "Get up," she gave him a swift kick to the forehead. The owner of the mill hurried in, picked up the senseless boy, and sent for Abe's father. Abe lay unconscious all night, and he was "apparently killed for a time." The next day, he started to regain consciousness, his frame jerked for an instant, and he awoke, blurting out the words "you old hussy!"

★ ★ ★

Being people of faith, Thomas and Sarah Lincoln became members of the Little Pigeon Creek Baptist Church. This was a "Hard Shell" or "Primitive" Baptist Church, whose beliefs were very conservative and Calvinistic. Abe attended church with his parents and held the position of sexton, responsible for maintenance of the church building.

Abe loved sitting in the room when adults were talking and would listen attentively to everything they said. His stepmother recalled that after everyone left, he would pepper his parents with questions, wanting to understand everything they had talked about. Abe would one day say that the only thing that ever made him angry was when an adult talked to him in such a way that he couldn't understand what they meant.

Abe had an opportunity to attend school again when he was about twelve years old and then again at fifteen. His sense of humor started showing up at this age, as a few surviving pages from one of his copy books demonstrate:

Abraham Lincoln
his hand and pen
he will be good
but god knows When

and

Abraham Lincoln is my nam[e]
And with my pen I wrote the same
I wrote in both hast[e] and speed
and left it here for fools to read.

His stepsister Matilda said that in addition to "ciphering" in copy books, Abe ciphered on just about everything else—including boards and walls when he didn't have paper.

Once, when Abe was reading aloud to Dennis and his stepmother from *The Arabian Nights* and *Aesop's Fables*, Dennis observed, "Abe, them yarns is all lies." Abe responded, "Mighty darn good lies, Denny," and continued with his reading. According to his cousin John Hanks, Abe "kept the Bible and *Aesop's Fables* always within reach, and read them over and over again." He would eventually commit many Psalms, Proverbs, and chapters of Isaiah to memory and state that the Bible was "the richest source of pertinent quotations."

Many would attest to Abe's ability to memorize. An acquaintance from Kentucky said that he was the "gawkiest, dullest looking boy you ever saw, unremarkable except for an exceptionally powerful memory." Rowan Herndon, who knew Abe when he was a young man, would say he "had the Best memory of any man I Ever Knew," for he "Never forgot anything he Read." Lincoln himself would later say that his mind was like a "piece of steel, very hard to scratch anything on it and almost impossible after you get it there to rub it out."

As he got older, Abe would walk miles to borrow books and obtained *Robinson Crusoe*, William Grimshaw's *History of the United States*, and William Scott's *Lessons in Elocution*. It was Scott's book that introduced Abe to Shakespeare—an author who would become a lifelong favorite.

Abe would become a gifted storyteller, but according to Cousin Dennis, his skill was nothing compared to that of his father. Thomas Lincoln could "beat his son telling a story—cracking a joke." One of the few surviving jokes attributed to Thomas was his response to his second wife Sarah, who asked which of his two wives he liked better, Nancy or her. Thomas replied, "Oh, now, Sally, that reminds me of old John Hardin down in Kentucky who had a fine looking pair of horses, and a neighbor coming in one day and looking at them said, 'John, which horse do you like the best?' John said, 'I can't tell; one of them kicks and the other bites and I don't know which is wust.'"

With his father as a role model, Abe's humor surfaced early in his life. One of the earliest recorded jokes that Abe told was when one of his neighbors, James Larkin, started bragging about his horse. He stepped up to Abe and commenced talking to him, boasting all the while of his animal.

"I have got the best horse in the country," he proclaimed to his young listener. "I ran him three miles in exactly nine minutes, and he never fetched a long breath."

"I presume," Abe responded dryly, "he fetched a good many short ones though."

In addition to showing him how to tell funny stories, Abe said that his father "learned him to work, but never to like it." Abe would frequently bring a book with him when going out to plant or harvest and during breaks would pull out his book and start to read. Dennis said that Abraham's father sometimes had to "slash him for neglecting his work by reading."

Abe's physical strength and stature made him very capable of all types of manual labor. Abe worked hard for his father, and as he got older, he grew to resent the way Thomas would hire him out to work for other farmers and then keep all of his wages. In referring to his youth, Lincoln would later say, with emotional hyperbole, that he "used to be a slave."

Hoping to get away from farm work, Abe developed many pastimes, including an increasing interest in public speaking. When he was a young teen, he liked to imitate the only good orators he had ever heard—preachers and traveling evangelists. Abe would pick up the family Bible and take his place behind an old tree stump while the children sat on the ground in front of him. He would begin by calling out a greeting and then reading some familiar scripture. He would next call for the first hymn, and the "congregation" would respond with some old John Newton or Isaac Watts hymn such as "Am I a soldier of the cross, a follower of the lamb..."

After finishing the hymn, Abe would repeat the sermon he had heard that morning, virtually word for word. Abe, who would one day say that when he saw a man preach, he liked to see him act as though he were "fighting bees," would walk back and forth in front of his congregation, imitating the mannerisms of the evangelist. As he preached, the children would cry out responses to his queries and shout a hearty "Amen!" when appropriate. Finally Abe would call for the last hymn and close with prayer.

While in his late teens, Abe would give political speeches, using what he had learned from a book on elocution as his guide. During breaks from farm work, he would stand on a stump and address his fellow workers until it was time to go back to work. Friends would later recall that he was a skilled public speaker even at that age and that he effectively used stories to make a point.

By the time Abe was seventeen, he was two inches shy of what would eventually be his full-grown height of six foot, four inches. Because of his size and strength, local farmers eagerly sought his help. But Abe wanted to do other work and began clerking in stores and chopping firewood for steamboats along the banks of the Ohio River.

In his late teens, Abe built a rowboat and began a business of ferrying passengers out to steamboats in the Ohio River. Once, two businessmen asked him to row them out to an approaching riverboat, and after he dropped them off, they each tossed a silver half-dollar into his boat. Abe would later recall that this was up till then "the most important incident of his life." He "could scarcely credit that [he], a poor boy, had earned a dollar in less than a day. The world seemed wider and fairer before [him]."

His ferrying business was probably the cause of Abe's first exposure to the courtroom. A businessman from the Kentucky side of the river sued him, claiming that Abe was not properly licensed. Abe went to court to defend himself, and the justice of the peace decided in his favor. This event may have been what stirred young Abe's interest in the law, for he started to read Constable Thomas Turnham's copy of *The Statutes of Indiana* shortly thereafter.

His interest in politics was also emerging, and after reading a biography of the politician Henry Clay of Kentucky, Abe became an admirer of Clay and later joined the Whig Party. Abe's stepmother noted that during this time, Abe also started avidly reading newspapers.

Abe had an interest in girls too but was incapable of relating to them on a romantic level. One evening, he was sitting with his friend Anna Roby, looking at the moon and stars. Abe had recently developed an interest in astronomy, and when Anna remarked that the moon was sinking, she recalled years later how Abe corrected her. "'That's not so,' he replied. 'It don't really go down; it seems so. The Earth turns from west to east and the revolution of the Earth carries us under, as it were; we do the sinking as you call it. The moon as to us is comparatively still. The moon's sinking is only an appearance.'"

Befuddled, Anna retorted, "Abe—what a fool you are."

Abe and his stepmother enjoyed a very close relationship, and she appreciated his sense of humor. Once, when she was not home, Abe spotted some children playing in the mud and got an idea for a joke. Abe took one of the toddlers into the cabin and helped him "walk" up the recently whitewashed wall and across the ceiling. When his stepmother saw the muddy footprints on her ceiling she laughed and threatened to spank him.

Abe had been blessed with a tragedy-free life for more than ten years, but when he was nineteen, his twenty-one-year-old sister Sarah died during childbirth. She had married neighbor Aaron Grigsby a year and a half earlier. The loss of his sister was a tremendous blow to Abe, and he always believed that her life, as well as the life of her son, might have been saved if the Grigsbys had sent for a doctor sooner.

Several months after the tragic loss of Sarah, Abe was given the opportunity to go on the biggest adventure of his life. A neighbor by the name of James Gentry hired him to accompany his son Allen on a flatboat Gentry intended to send to New Orleans to sell livestock and produce. Around the first of the year, 1829, the young men pushed out into the Ohio River with their cargo. The trip took three months and was of immense educational benefit to Abe, who turned twenty while traveling to New Orleans. In that city, he got his first up-close look at slavery, and when he saw how human beings were bought and sold, he called it "a disgrace." He returned home via steamboat, having earned the sum of twenty-four dollars, which his father, of course, kept.

Although Abe resented his father's tightfisted habits and disdain for education, he remained faithful to his family. Even though he had turned the legal age of twenty-one and could leave his family, he stayed with them when Thomas decided to sell his Indiana farm and move to Illinois in early

1830. Abe dutifully helped pack the family belongings into an oxcart and move to the Prairie State. He helped them establish a new homestead near Decatur, Illinois, by erecting a cabin and barn, splitting enough rails to fence fifteen acres, and planting a crop.

In the spring of 1831, at the age of twenty-two, Abe prepared to make another trip to New Orleans via flatboat. This time, he, his stepbrother John D. Johnston, and cousin John Hanks made the trip under the employment of a businessman named Denton Offutt. After constructing the flatboat, they began their journey at Springfield, Illinois, and in April started down the Sangamon River with Offutt's goods. They had not gotten far, however, when their flatboat got hung up on a milldam at New Salem, Illinois. Unable to dislodge the boat, it quickly began to fill up with water. Abe drilled a hole in the front of the boat, which was hanging over the dam, in order to drain the water. He then helped his companions redistribute their cargo, and the boat successfully slipped over the dam. This quick thinking impressed not only Offutt but the residents of New Salem as well, who had gathered along the banks of the Sangamon to witness the excitement.

Offutt had plans to open a store in New Salem and told Abe he could have a job as a clerk when he returned from the trip to New Orleans. Upon his return, Abe made a brief visit to say good-bye to his parents and then set out for New Salem. It was the summer of 1831.

A PIECE OF FLOATING DRIFTWOOD
1831–1842

The village of New Salem was situated along the banks of the Sangamon River in the central part of the state and had about a hundred hearty souls residing in its fifteen or twenty cabins. Lincoln, who arrived by way of the Sangamon River, would later say that he came to New Salem "like a piece of floating driftwood." He joked that the river was so meandering and serpentine that while traveling on it, "he had camped at the same place three nights in a row."

True to his promise, Denton Offutt hired Lincoln to help build and manage a general store. After helping Offutt cut the logs, construct the store, and stock it with general merchandise, Lincoln settled in his job of selling goods.

Lincoln was happy to finally be out on his own, and as a store clerk, he quickly made a lot of friends. He loved to swap stories, tell jokes, and do small favors for people. One local, Clark E. Carr, said that Lincoln was "the most comical and jocose of human beings, laughing with the same zest at his own jokes as at those of others." Carr added that he had never seen "another who provoked so much mirth, and who entered into rollicking fun with such glee. He could make a cat laugh."

Lincoln also gained the trust of the townspeople. The local schoolmaster, Mentor Graham, recalled that Lincoln "was among the best clerks [he] ever saw. [Lincoln] was attentive to his business—was kind and considerate to his customers and friends and always treated them with great tenderness, kindness, and honesty." Another resident, Robert B. Rutledge, attested to Lincoln's character, saying, "People relied implicitly upon his honesty, integrity, and impartiality."

Lincoln possessed a great deal of self-confidence and was quite comfortable telling jokes that ridiculed his own appearance. Typical of these, Lincoln said that he was surprised one day by a scowling man who drew a revolver and thrust the weapon into Lincoln's face. He swallowed hard and quickly decided that any attempt at argument might be the last thing he ever did.

"What seems to be the matter?" inquired Lincoln with all the calmness and self-possession he could muster.

"'Well,' replied the stranger, who did not appear at all excited, 'some years ago I swore an oath that if I ever came across a man uglier than myself I'd shoot him on the spot.'

"A feeling of relief evidently took possession of Lincoln at this rejoinder, as the expression upon his countenance lost all suggestion of anxiety. 'Shoot me,' he said to the stranger, 'for if I am uglier than you, I don't want to live!'"

Lincoln's stature, strength, and athletic ability were other traits that made him popular with the people of the region. Soon after arriving in New Salem, he demonstrated his physical prowess by wrestling a local bully, Jack Armstrong. Doing well in this contest, he won the respect of Armstrong and his friends, who were known as the Clary's Grove Boys. In them and those watching the contest, Lincoln developed an army of allies. Lincoln's future law partner John Todd Stuart said that this contest was a "turning point in Lincoln's life."

Lincoln was a keen student of human nature and formed deep friendships with many people. Once, while Lincoln was talking with a few friends about human faults, the subject of greed came up. This reminded Lincoln of a story about a hog:

> A man in Cortlandt county raised a porker of such unusual size that strangers went out of their way to see it. One of them the other day met the old gentleman and inquired about the animal.
>
> "Waal, yes," the old fellow said; "I've got such a critter, mi'ty big un; but I guess I'll have to charge you about a shilling for lookin' at him."
>
> The surprised stranger stared at the old man for a minute, pulled out the desired coin, handed it to him and started to go off. "Hold on," said the other; "don't you want to see the hog?"

"No," said the stranger; "I've already seen as big a hog as
I ever want to see!"

But Lincoln was interested in much more than human nature—he was
an avid student of many subjects. When he wasn't laughing and swapping
yarns, clerking the store, or running errands for people, he was studying.
Lincoln's ravenous appetite for reading never waned, and in New Salem,
he studied subjects such as arithmetic, philosophy, astronomy, history,
poetry, and Shakespeare. His favorite poet was Robert Burns, and he especially loved Shakespeare's *Hamlet* and *Macbeth*.

With the help of his schoolmaster friend Mentor Graham and a copy
of Samuel Kirkham's *English Grammar in Familiar Lectures*, he tackled
subjects he had received little instruction in, like grammar and speech.
Interested in improving his skill at public speaking, Lincoln joined the
New Salem debating society, which helped him prepare for future courtroom presentations and political speeches.

Lincoln also continued his interest in law. He attended sessions of
the local court, which was presided over by Justice of the Peace Bowling
Green. Appreciating Lincoln's sense of humor, Green would occasionally
ask Lincoln to make informal comments on cases before the court, which
inevitably resulted in a "spasmodic shaking of the fat sides of the old law
functionary." In addition to amusing the judge, however, Lincoln proved
he had serious intentions in the courtroom as well. Some of the locals

began to rely on Lincoln, the nascent student of law, for legal advice. He acquired a book of legal forms and began drafting simple deeds and receipts for people.

Once, in Green's court, Lincoln was called on by plaintiff Pete Lukins's lawyer to attest to the validity of his client's oath. The attorney said to Lincoln, "Please state what you know as to the character of Mr. Lukins as for truth and veracity."

"Well," said Lincoln, "he's called *lying* Pete Lukins."

Somewhat taken aback, the lawyer responded, "But, would you believe him on oath?"

Lincoln turned around and said, "Ask Esquire Green. He's taken his testimony under oath many times."

Green was asked the same question by the lawyer and the justice of the peace answered, "I never believe anything he says unless somebody else swears the same thing."

Although Lincoln had been raised by religious parents and would one day be a man of deep

The Railsplitter by Jean Leon Gerome Ferris

faith himself, he had become more of a religious skeptic and had no reservations about telling funny stories involving preachers and church life.
One was about the preacher who proclaimed, during his sermon, that
"although the Lord was the only perfect man, the Bible never mentioned
a perfect woman."

A woman in the rear of the congregation called out, "I know a perfect
woman, and I've heard of her every day for the last six years."

"Who was she?" asked the surprised minister.

"My husband's first wife," came the reply.

At the encouragement of friends, Lincoln decided to run for the state
legislature in March 1832. This was a timely decision, because the store
where Lincoln clerked had recently failed. So at the age of twenty-three,
Lincoln became a candidate for the lower house of the state legislature.

Lincoln announced his candidacy and political platform in the *Sangamo
Journal* on March 9, 1832. In this announcement, Lincoln wisely avoided
controversial national issues and stuck to popular subjects. He announced
he was in favor of various public works such as improvements to the
Sangamon River and the construction of roads, canals, and railroads.
Conscious of his own lack of schooling, he said that he believed everyone
should be provided at least a moderate level of education so that they could
"read the Scriptures and other works."

He concluded his announcement of candidacy by proclaiming:

Every man is said to have his peculiar ambition. Whether it be true or not, I can say for one that I have no other so great as that of being truly esteemed of my fellow men, by rendering myself worthy of their esteem. How far I shall succeed in gratifying this ambition, is yet to be developed. I am young and unknown to many of you. I was born and have ever remained in the most humble walks of life. I have no wealthy or popular relations to recommend me. My case is thrown exclusively upon the independent voters of this county, and if elected they will have conferred a favor upon me, for which I shall be unremitting in my labors to compensate. But if the good people in their wisdom shall see fit to keep me in the background, I have been too familiar with disappointments to be very much chagrined.

Shortly after announcing his decision to run, Lincoln's campaign was interrupted by his state's call for volunteers to serve in the militia. Sauk Indian chief Black Hawk, along with about five hundred Sauk, Meskwaki, and Kickapoo Indian warriors, had crossed the Mississippi River from Iowa into Illinois. They hoped to resettle on land they believed they had been swindled out of.

Lincoln postponed his political campaign and joined a militia unit to help repulse Black Hawk. Much to his surprise, he was elected captain by his men—something he would say, more than twenty years later, was "a success that gave me more pleasure than I have had since." With the assistance of Jack Armstrong, his first sergeant, Lincoln did his best to instill some discipline in his men, including the rowdy Clary's Grove Boys. When he gave his first order to one of the men, he responded with "go to the Devil, sir!"

One of his responsibilities as captain was to lead his men in close order drill. But Lincoln's military parading skills were rather slim. While leading his men, he marched them toward a fence that had a narrow gate in it. Lincoln suddenly realized he couldn't remember the command that would successfully pass them single file through the gate. At the last minute, he ordered them to halt and then shouted, "This company is dismissed for two minutes, when it will fall in agin' on the other side of the gate!"

Captain Lincoln had some difficulty keeping his raw troops in order. On one occasion, some of Lincoln's men got drunk and disorderly, incurring the wrath of Lincoln's superiors. As punishment, the young captain was forced to carry a large wooden sword for two days.

Lincoln and his men joined a force that had been ordered to find Black Hawk. They spent weeks trying to track him down, and never even got a glimpse of someone vaguely resembling an enemy until an old drunken Potawatomi Indian stumbled into their camp. Several of Lincoln's men wanted to kill him, claiming that he was a spy. Lincoln stood in front of the old man and said that anyone who wanted to harm him would have to fight him first. When they told him they didn't believe he would fight, he said, "Try me." The old Indian left camp, unharmed.

After a few weeks, Lincoln's initial enlistment expired. Having no other employment, he decided to enlist for another term as a private and was sworn in by Lieutenant Robert Anderson, whom Lincoln would meet again during the Civil War. After his second term was over, he reenlisted for a third term before the war ended. Three months after his original enlistment, Lincoln returned to his political campaign, having never seen the enemy.

In July 1832, Lincoln held his first campaign rally in the village of Pappsville, Illinois. A fight broke out in the audience just as he was about to begin his speech. Noticing that his friend J. Rowan Herndon was getting whipped by a gang of men, Lincoln cut his way through the crowd and pitched in with Herndon. He threw several of Herndon's assailants about as if they were mere boys, tossing the one that had Herndon down ten or twelve feet. This ended the fight, and Lincoln returned to the platform to give his speech to the admiring audience. One onlooker recalled that his speech went something like this:

> Fellow citizens, I suppose you all know who I am. I am humble Abraham Lincoln. I have been solicited by many friends to become a candidate for the Legislature. My politics are short and sweet, like the old woman's dance. I am in favor of a

national bank. I am in favor of the internal-improvement system and a high protective tariff. These are my sentiments and political principles. If elected I shall be thankful; if not it will be all the same.

Although Lincoln won overwhelmingly in his own precinct, collecting 277 out of 300 votes, he lost the election because he was unknown in other precincts. He would later say that this was the only time he was ever defeated in a political contest by the direct vote of the people. The political contests he lost in the future, for the U.S. Senate, were a result of tallies in the Illinois legislature rather than the voters.

After losing the election, Lincoln went into partnership with village resident William Berry and opened another general store in New Salem. Again Lincoln worked dutifully behind the counter, selling goods, telling stories, and swapping jokes, but Berry drank up all the profits. This store failed too, and when Berry died a couple of years after the start of the partnership, Lincoln was left with a debt of $1,100. This sum, which he referred to as his "national debt," would take him fifteen years to pay off.

After the Berry store "winked out," Lincoln's friends helped him secure an appointment as postmaster of New Salem in May 1833. Lincoln was delighted to have this job, despite the low pay, because it gave him access to all of the newspapers. The modest income of postmaster proved insufficient to cover his bills, so Lincoln obtained a copy of Robert Gibson's

Theory and Practice of Surveying and taught himself a new trade. He soon became deputy surveyor and worked part time in New Salem and surrounding communities. Surveying allowed him to travel to various parts of the county, make more friends, and learn the art of settling disputes between neighbors.

While working as postmaster and surveyor, Lincoln diligently studied law. He read Blackstone's *Commentaries* and the *Revised Laws of Illinois* and continued to plead minor cases before Bowling Green. Through experience in the justice of the peace's court and the New Salem debating society, Lincoln improved both his knowledge of the law and his speaking skills.

Undeterred by his previous defeat, Lincoln decided to run for the state legislature again in 1834. More widely known now, he secured the support of both the Democratic and the recently formed Whig parties. This time he was successful, and on August 4, he was elected representative from Sangamon County. With this rise in stature, Lincoln became more conscious of his physical appearance. Since he would be making the phenomenal salary of four dollars per day, he bought his first suit for sixty dollars, and on December 1, he traveled to the state capital of Vandalia to take his seat in the Illinois General Assembly.

The purchase of a new suit was a major event for Lincoln, as he had never been concerned about his clothes. He once saw a show where the magician asked for a volunteer from the audience to loan him a hat.

Although he was reluctant to do so, Lincoln finally handed over his old hat, which the showman used to fry eggs in. When given the hat back, Lincoln said, "Mister, the reason I didn't give you my hat before was out of respect for your eggs—not care for my hat."

Lincoln was, however, an expert at finding the usefulness in clothes, beyond just being for warmth and comfort. Once, while walking to Springfield, he pretended to show concern for his coat. When a gentleman in a buggy drove up, Lincoln asked him, "Will you have the goodness to take my overcoat to town for me?"

"With pleasure," replied the stranger, "but how will you get it again?"

"Oh, very readily," said Lincoln. "I intend to remain in it."

During his first term in the state legislature, Lincoln was fortunate enough to share a room with fellow Whig and minority leader John Todd Stuart. Stuart liked Lincoln very much and took time to teach his protégé as much as he could about the practical functioning of the state legislature. Stuart taught Lincoln how to write bills, introduce them, and maneuver them through the assembly.

Even though Lincoln did not deliver any speeches in his first term, he was appointed to about a dozen special committees. He developed a love for politics, in spite of the fact that he was a member of the minority party.

In Illinois, the Whigs were significantly outnumbered by the Democrats, but Lincoln refused to give in to the temptation to switch parties, as many less-principled men did. To Lincoln, Whigs stood for economic progress and upward mobility for the underprivileged, whereas the Democrats were for maintaining a backward, agriculture-based economy.

Back in New Salem, Lincoln developed his first love interest, a pretty and quick-witted girl named Ann Rutledge. She was pursued by all the community's eligible bachelors, but it soon became known that she was to marry John McNeil, a boarder at the Rutledge Tavern. After this understanding had been reached, however, McNeil told Ann that his real name was John McNamar, and he had to leave New Salem to go back east and clear up some family business before they could marry. In McNamar's absence, Lincoln and Ann became close, and it is believed that they decided to marry sometime after Ann sent word to McNamar that she was no longer interested in him.

Tragically, on August 25, 1835, Ann died of typhoid. Lincoln plunged into such deep depression that friends feared he would take his own life. Lincoln called these bouts of depression "the hypo," which was short for hypochondriasis. He moved in with his surrogate father Bowling Green for a while, but the passage of time and his return to books, jokes, and stories finally got him through.

In August 1836, Lincoln was again elected to the state legislature, which assembled in December. In this second term, he met the man who would become his lifelong political nemesis, Stephen A. Douglas. A Democrat from Jacksonville, Illinois, Douglas was a skilled lawyer and speaker who would one day develop a national reputation in politics. In the coming years, Lincoln would oppose Douglas in the legislature, compete with him for the hand of a young lady, work both with and against him in the court-room, and run against him for the U.S. Senate and the presidency.

Lincoln's oratorical skills improved during his second term as a legisla-tor, and he became a confident floor speaker for the Whig Party. He used storytelling to overcome his nervousness, and it was not long before both Democrats and Whigs realized that when Lincoln rose to speak, there would be a good chuckle. During a debate with another legislator from Wabash County, who was known for his large, bushy eyebrows and his tendency to make "big bugaboos" about small problems, Lincoln couldn't resist poking fun at these peculiar characteristics of his opponent:

> Mister Speaker, the attack of the member from Wabash on the constitutionality of this measure reminds me of an ol' friend-a-mine. He's a peculiar looking old fellow, with shaggy, overhanging eye-brows, and a pair of spectacles under them.

One morning just after the old man got up, he imagined, on lookin' out his door, that he saw a rather lively squirrel on a tree near his house. So he took down his rifle and fired at the squirrel, but the critter paid no attention to the shot. He loaded and fired ag'in and ag'in. After the thirteenth shot, he set down his gun impatiently, and said to his boy, who was looking on, "Boy there's something wrong 'bout this rifle."

"Rifle's all right, I know, 'tis," replied the boy, "but whar's your squirrel?"

"Don't you see him, humped up 'bout half way up the tree?" inquired the old man, peeping over his spectacles, and getting mystified.

"No, I don't," responded the boy; and then turning and looking into his father's face he exclaimed, "I see your squirrel! You've been firing at a louse on your eyebrow!"

Lincoln then claimed that his opponent had been doing the same thing in attacking his bill.

Lincoln and the eight other Whig legislators from Sangamon County were a tall bunch, with an average height between them of more than six feet. One Democratic newspaper derisively referred to them as "the Long Nine," and the nickname stuck. One of the most noteworthy accomplishments of the Long Nine was to get the state capital of Illinois moved from

Vandalia to Springfield, a bill they successfully secured the passage of in late February 1837.

When he was twenty-eight years old, Lincoln first spoke out against the institution of slavery. A bill had been introduced that condemned the formation of abolition societies, and Lincoln, along with one other member of the legislature, voted against it. The two representatives boldly stated that "the institution of slavery is founded on both injustice and bad policy," but they also demonstrated that they were not completely satisfied with abolitionists either when they added "but the promulgation of abolition doctrines tends rather to increase than to abate its [slavery's] evils."

In the spring of 1837, Lincoln was admitted to the Illinois bar, and his mentor, John Todd Stuart, accepted Lincoln as junior partner in his law practice. Becoming junior partner was a big break for Lincoln, because Stuart ran one of the most successful law practices in Springfield.

Now that he was a practicing attorney, Lincoln decided to leave New Salem and take up residence in Springfield. After his second term in the legislature ended, he moved in with a Springfield merchant by the name of Joshua Speed. Having brought all of his worldly possessions in two saddlebags, he took them upstairs to Speed's room, set them on the floor, and quickly came back. "Well, Speed, I'm moved," he announced.

Lincoln wasn't interested in just law and politics. Throughout his twenties, he continued his bumbling pursuit of the opposite sex. He said that women were "the only things that cannot hurt me that I am afraid of." One young woman, Martinette Hardin, said that he was "so awkward that[she] was always sorry for him." He "did not seem to know what to say in the company of women."

In 1838, Lincoln wrote a letter to his friend Mrs. Orville H. Browning about his second romance (after Ann Rutledge). Her name was Mary Owens, and at the time of Lincoln's writing, Mary lived in Kentucky. Lincoln had met her three years earlier when she visited her sister in New Salem. Somehow the subject of matrimony came up when he was talking to Mary's sister and Lincoln said that he had "no good objection to plodding life through, hand-in-hand with her," if Mary was interested. In no time, Lincoln was informed that Mary Owens was returning to New Salem. In his letter to Browning, Lincoln described his reacquaintance with Mary when she came back to Illinois, marriage minded:

> In a few days we had an interview, and although I had seen her before, she did not look as my imagination had pictured her. I knew she was over-size, but she now appeared a fair match for Falstaff; I knew she was called an "old maid," and I felt no doubt of the truth of at least half of the appellation; but now, when I beheld her, I could not for my life avoid thinking of my mother; and this, not from withered features, for her skin was too full of fat to permit its contracting in to wrinkles; but from her want of teeth, weather-beaten

appearance in general, and from a kind of notion that ran in my head, that nothing could have commenced at the size of infancy, and reached her present bulk in less than thirty-five or forty years; and, in short, I was not all pleased with her.

Feeling obligated to marry her, Lincoln began a reluctant courtship of Mary. It did not take long, however, for her to realize that he was not the man for her. Later saying that Lincoln lacked "those little links which make up the great chain of woman's happiness," she broke off their relationship and returned home to Kentucky. Lincoln told Browning "others have been made fools of by the girls, but this can never with truth be said of me. I most emphatically, in this instance, made a fool of myself."

Lincoln grew rather despondent over his inability to find a wife and wrote, "I have now come to the conclusion never again to think of marrying, and for this reason; I can never be satisfied with anyone who would be blockhead enough to have me."

In the fall of 1838, Lincoln was reelected to the Illinois General Assembly and returned to Vandalia for his third term in early December. In this term, he became a more prominent leader because his partner John Todd Stuart had left the state legislature for a seat in the U.S. House of Representatives in Washington, DC. Although Lincoln lost a bid for Speaker of the House, he became the de facto floor leader for the Whigs and was appointed to the legislature's finance committee.

A great deal of his efforts in the finance committee involved the defense of the Illinois state bank against attacks by the Democrats, who wanted to close it. Lincoln, while arguing against a Democratic party effort to defeat the state bank, attacked his opponents' credibility in the following manner: "Mister Cheerman, this work is exclusively the work of politicians; a set of men who have interests aside from the interests of the people, and who, to say the most of them, are, taken as a mass, at least one long step removed from honest men. I say this with the greater freedom because, bein' a politician myself, none can regard it as personal."

In 1839, Lincoln met his future wife, Mary Todd. Mary was a well-educated young lady from a wealthy, slave-holding Kentucky family and the cousin of John Todd Stuart. She had recently moved to Springfield to live with her sister and brother-in-law, Elizabeth and Ninian Edwards. The Edwards home had become a sort of social center of town and was frequented by most of the town's young bachelors, including Lincoln.

Mary Todd was very interested in politics and made no secret of her desire to marry the man who would one day be president. Although she had the attention of many of the town's bachelors, including Stephen A. Douglas, she soon fell in love with the tallest and homeliest of the lot, Abraham Lincoln. Douglas had proposed marriage to Mary, but they did not see eye to eye, in spite of being of similar height. She was a devoted Whig and he a dyed-in-the-wool Democrat. Douglas, after being rejected, told her that she had "thrown away" her best chance to "rule in the White House."

According to Elizabeth Edwards, who considered Lincoln unworthy of her sister's attention, it was comical to watch the young couple when they were together. They would sit on the sofa in the Edwards's parlor, and while Mary breathlessly chattered on, rapidly switching from subject to subject, Lincoln would sit in silence with a dumbfounded look on his face. Lincoln, the quick-witted storyteller who was so comfortable in the company of men, was absolutely tongue tied in the presence of this spirited, sophisticated young lady. Mary Todd once recounted that at one of her parties, Lincoln approached her and told her he wanted to dance with her "in the worst way." She later said that is exactly what he did—he danced "in the worst way." The awkward Lincoln, over a foot taller than Mary, cutting a rug with the petite young lady who had graduated from Madame Mantelle's Finishing School must have presented a ludicrous sight. But love is blind, and in 1840, Lincoln and Mary became engaged.

Shortly after their engagement, Lincoln was elected to his fourth term in the legislature and took his seat in December 1840. Thanks to the effort of the Long Nine, the state capital was now in Springfield, and the legislature met in temporary quarters at the Methodist Episcopal Church. On December 5, Lincoln and the Whigs wanted to prevent a quorum so that the lower house would not be able to vote on an issue regarding the state bank. Accordingly, Lincoln directed that, with the exception of himself and a few others, all Whigs absent themselves. The Democrats discovered the ruse and sent the sergeant at arms to bring in the missing members. He returned without the necessary number, so the Democrats locked the doors to prevent the escape of the Whigs already present. Suddenly a number of Democrats who, due to illness, had not been present appeared and a quorum was unexpectedly announced. Caught by surprise, Lincoln and his fellows attempted to escape. Finding the doors locked, they went into a panic, opened a window, and jumped out.

Lincoln and Mary's relationship became a stormy one in the latter months of the year, and on the first of January, 1841, Lincoln broke off their engagement. Disappointing Mary threw Lincoln into a long bout of depression, which adversely impacted his performance as a floor leader for the Whigs. This opened the door for the opportunistic Stephen A. Douglas to attain a position as judge on the Illinois Supreme Court.

In between sessions of the state legislature, which typically lasted only two or three months, Lincoln continued to earn his living as a lawyer. In 1841, Lincoln and John T. Stuart had an amicable parting of ways, and Lincoln became junior partner to another established lawyer, Stephen A. Logan.

Logan was of Irish descent and enjoyed Lincoln's courtroom stories involving Irish characters, such as the Irish sailor who had been overtaken at sea by a heavy storm. The sailor thought he ought to pray but didn't know how. So he fell to his knees and said, "Oh Lord! Ye know as well as meself that it's seldom I bodder ye, but if ye will only hear me and save me this time, bedad it will be a long time before I bodder ye again."

Lincoln and Mary started seeing each other again in 1842. Lincoln, however, remained uncertain about matrimony and questioned whether he and Mary would be happy together. He decided to write his old friend Joshua Speed, who had moved to Kentucky and recently married, asking, "Are you now in feeling, as well as judgment, glad you are married as you are?" He wanted his old friend to "answer it quickly," as he was "impatient to know."

Speed assured him that "happiness would be the result of his marriage to Miss Todd."

Once the young couple made up their mind to marry, they did it quickly. The morning of November 4, Mary announced to her sister that she was going to marry Lincoln that evening. Elizabeth was flabbergasted at the short notice but insisted that the wedding take place in her home. Lincoln arranged a minister, Reverend Charles N. Dresser, and took some time to make himself more presentable. While blackening his boots, a friend asked Lincoln where he was going. "To hell, I reckon," he replied.

Elizabeth hastily made what arrangements she could, buying gingerbread and beer for the reception. The wedding party consisted of two groomsmen and two bridesmaids. The guests included the opinionated, portly old state supreme court justice Thomas C. Brown. When Lincoln repeated the vow "with this ring, I thee endow with all my goods and chattels, lands and tenements," Justice Brown blurted out, "Lord Almighty, Lincoln, the Statute fixes all that!" Reverend Dresser managed to stifle a guffaw, compose himself, and pronounce Lincoln and Mary husband and wife.

Shortly afterward, Lincoln casually mentioned the event in a letter to his friend Samuel D. Marshall. "Nothing new here, except my marrying. Which to me, is a matter of profound wonder."

GOING TO CONGRESS
1842-1849

Lincoln had finally found—and fallen in love with—the woman who was "blockhead enough" to marry him. Although Mary Todd was educated, well mannered, and accustomed to having many of the finer things of life, she was not above making sacrifices as a young wife to help them get on their feet. The first year of their marriage, they had room and board for four dollars a week at the unremarkable Globe Tavern in Springfield. Following the custom of the day, as a respectable young wife, Mary did not work outside of the home.

In the fall of 1842, Lincoln was nearly involved in a duel with James Shields, the state auditor. Lincoln had published some anonymous letters ridiculing Shields in the *Sangamo Journal*, and Shields demanded to know their source. When Lincoln acknowledged himself as author, the diminutive Shields challenged him to a duel. Lincoln proposed cavalry broadswords "of the largest size" as weapons, and on his way to the duel site, he wisecracked that the situation brought to mind a story of a Kentuckian who volunteered for service in the War of 1812. As he was about to leave home for the war, his sweetheart presented him a bullet pouch and belt she had embroidered with the motto: "Victory or Death." In expressing his gratitude, the young man said, "Isn't that rather too strong? Suppose you put 'Victory or Be Crippled?'" Friends intervened and the duel was avoided, but it remained one of the most embarrassing incidents of Lincoln's life.

Mary soon became pregnant, and their first child, Robert Todd Lincoln, was born on August 1, 1843. Lincoln joked that he was relieved to see the baby, because he had been afraid that Robert might be born with a long leg from his father and a short one from his mother, which would result in him having "a terrible time getting through the world."

By this time, Lincoln was doing better financially, so he rented a house on south Fourth Street and hired some part-time domestic help for Mary. He soon found that to hire domestic help for his wife was one thing, but to keep the help was quite another. Perhaps it was her aristocratic upbringing, or maybe because of severe headaches, but Mary would frequently get so angry with her maids that they would quit in tears. On at least one occasion, Lincoln offered to pay a girl under the table an additional twenty-five cents a week in wages to make it worth her while to endure his wife.[1]

While Lincoln was putting his political career on hold, his once and future antagonist Stephen A. Douglas's career was taking off. Douglas had left the Illinois General Assembly behind in 1841, become a state supreme

1. Offer to pay additional wages from Wilson and Davis, *Herndon's Informants*, 445.

court justice, and in March 1843, took his seat in the U.S. House of Representatives as Democratic representative from Illinois's Fifth Congressional District. Lincoln wanted to go to Congress too, but the Illinois Whig Party only controlled one seat in that body, the Seventh District of Springfield. There were many popular Whig nominees, so in order to give himself a chance, Lincoln worked out a deal that would arrange for him and two other senior Whig

Mary Todd Lincoln

politicians to take turns running for Congress. Lincoln was to be the third, which meant he had to wait until 1846 for his next political campaign.

In the fall of 1844, Lincoln decided to end his partnership with Stephen A. Logan and open his own law practice. He hired twenty-five-year-old William Herndon, a promising lawyer and influential man among the younger Whigs, as junior partner.

Also in 1844, Lincoln bought an attractive, one-and-a-half-story house at the corner of Eighth and Jackson streets in Springfield. Costing $1,500,

Earliest known photograph of Abraham Lincoln

it was the only house he ever owned. Once the Lincolns were settled into their new house, Mary took a keener interest in sprucing up her husband's appearance. Since he was now a successful lawyer, she tried her best to improve his social manners as well as his manner of dress. She lectured Lincoln on proper attire for receiving visitors and encouraged him to let the servants answer the door. Her exasperation skyrocketed one day when she realized he had personally answered the door in his stocking feet and told the visitor that his wife was upstairs but would be down "as soon as she got all her trotting harness on."

Mary was often frustrated with the chores of cooking, cleaning, and taking care of an infant. Although Lincoln was more than willing to provide part-time help for Mary, his work as a lawyer demanded a great deal of his time. It was not possible to generate enough income from legal work in Springfield alone, so twice a year, he would travel the Eighth Circuit with Judge Davis and a gaggle of lawyers. The spring term usually started in mid-March, and the fall term in early September. While Lincoln was on these extended trips, Herndon ran the office and took care of legal affairs in Springfield.

Senator Fred T. Dubois, who was a child when he knew Lincoln, recalled that the neighborhood children loved to play pranks on the future president when he was on his way home from work. Dubois said, "When Mr. Lincoln, with his arms folded behind his back and evidently in deep thought, would be suddenly aroused by having his hat knocked off by some unseen power, we would raise a mighty yell, rush out from our hiding places, grab hold of him wherever we could find a place, and shout for joy. All his serious thoughts would vanish instantly and he would laugh and romp with us, and not infrequently march up the street with all the boys clinging around him until he could find a place to buy us some nuts or fruit."

Lincoln and Mary both loved children and were overjoyed when their second son, Edward Baker, was born on March 10, 1846. Eddie, as he was called, was named after Lincoln's longtime friend and political associate Edward Dickinson Baker.

The addition of little Eddie did not make things easier for Mary. Sometimes Mary would tell her husband to take the boys out of the house, presumably for her own sanity, and Lincoln would oblige by putting them in a wagon and pulling them down the street while he read a book. Once a neighbor related an instance where Lincoln had become so absorbed in his book, he didn't realize that one of the boys had fallen out of the wagon and was crying in the street until he was some distance away.

In 1846, Lincoln's turn to run for Congress finally arrived. His Democratic opponent for the Seventh District was a famous Methodist preacher and evangelist, Peter Cartwright. Cartwright decided that the fact Lincoln was not a member of any church would make a good political point he could press to advantage and attacked Lincoln on the grounds of religious infidelity.

Responding to this attack, Lincoln printed a handbill statement on July 31. In it, he acknowledged that he was not a church member but added, "I have never denied the truth of the Scriptures; and I have never spoken with intentional disrespect of religion in general, or of any denomination of Christians in particular." He concluded, "I do not think I could myself, be brought to support a man for office, whom I knew to be an open enemy of, and scoffer at, religion."

There is a popular story of an interchange between the two candidates in church during the campaign. Lincoln went to listen to one of Cartwright's sermons and sat in a back pew. At the end of the sermon, Cartwright asked everyone who wanted to go to heaven to stand up. Lincoln remained sitting. Cartwright then asked everyone who wanted to go to hell to stand up. Lincoln remained sitting. Finally, singling Lincoln out, Cartwright said, "May I inquire of you, Mr. Lincoln, where you are going?"

"I am going to Congress," was Lincoln's reply.

Fortunately, the Whig Party had a strong majority in the district, so he easily defeated Cartwright in the election on August 3, although he would not take his seat in Congress until late the following year.

In 1846, the nation's attention was focused on the Mexican-American War. In May of that year, Democratic president James K. Polk declared war on Mexico over the annexation of Texas. Lincoln saw this as blatant aggression on the part of the Democratic leadership in Washington and did not approve of the United States using its greater strength to take land from a weaker neighbor.

Finally it was time for Lincoln to go to Congress, so in November 1847, he packed up Mary and their children—four-year-old Robert and one-and-a-half-year-old Eddie—and headed for Washington, DC. Once there, they moved in to Mrs. Sprigg's Boarding House, a popular residence for junior congressman that stood on the present-day site of the Jefferson Building of the Library of Congress. The Sprigg house did not host many families with children, so life there was not a very happy one for Mary. She did not get along well with many of the residents, usually stayed in their one-room apartment during the day with the boys, and rarely came downstairs for anything except meals.

Lincoln took his seat in the Thirtieth Congress on December 6, 1847. Although the Thirtieth Congress was filled with the usual assortment of incompetents, miscreants, and party hacks, there were a few men of legitimate ability whom Lincoln would develop a genuine respect for. Among these was the future vice president of the Confederacy, Alexander H. Stephens, from Georgia. Stephens, a fellow Whig, would be an ally of Lincoln's on several issues in Congress, the most notable of which was their mutual opposition to the Mexican-American War.

The Mexican-American War was still raging when Lincoln arrived in Washington, and soon after taking his seat, Lincoln criticized President Polk in a series of floor speeches which became known as the "spot" resolutions. In these, he tried to force the president to say whether the "spot" where American troops were first fired upon by Mexican forces was on U.S. soil. Polk ignored the freshman congressman's questions, but Lincoln's constituents of the Seventh District in Illinois did not. The Springfield Democrats accused Lincoln of not supporting the troops, calling him "spotty" Lincoln. Although this was not true, Lincoln's reputation suffered back home.

Mary and her rambunctious boys continued to have trouble getting along with the residents of the boardinghouse. Within three months of arriving in Washington, Mary and Lincoln decided that for the sake of peace and quiet at the Sprigg establishment, it might be best for Mary and the boys to go live with the Todd family in Kentucky. So Lincoln put them on a train and sent them to his in-laws.

During one of his subsequent letters to Mary in Kentucky, Lincoln wrote that "all the house—or rather, all with whom you were on decided good terms—send their love to you. The others say nothing."

While Mary and the children were in Kentucky, Lincoln led a lonely life in Washington. Never one for drinking or gambling, the usual vices of congressmen, Lincoln went bowling. Although he didn't wear his tall hat and tails, he nevertheless drew a crowd. In between turns, he amused his companions with jokes and stories.

Lincoln worked hard while in Congress, and his wit, good nature, and humor soon won him many friends from both the Whig and Democratic sides of the aisle. He faithfully accomplished party assignments, gave speeches, and performed countless favors for constituents. With the exception of his 1849 bill to ban slavery in the District of Columbia, he did little that was historically noteworthy. This bill would have taken the moderate approach of gradually abolishing slavery, but it never became law. As a freshman Whig congressman, he was not able to assemble enough support to make formal submission of the bill worthwhile.

Lincoln said that he was always embarrassed when he got up to talk, and this was as true in Congress as anywhere else. He said that he "felt like the boy whose teacher asked him why he didn't spell better. The boy replied: 'Cause I hain't just got the hang of the school-house, but I'll get on better later.'"

Although he might have been nervous, Lincoln was quite successful at using his speaking skills to lampoon the Polk administration and other Democrats on political issues. Lincoln said that the Democrats' claim that the Mexican-American War was *not* a ploy to get new territory reminded him of the farmer who asserted, "I ain't greedy 'bout land, I only jus wants what jines [joins] mine."

There is no better example of Lincoln's political wit while in the House of Representatives than his speech of July 27, 1848. He started by addressing Democrats who had accused Whigs of clinging to the coattails of Zachary Taylor in the presidential election. Taylor was running against the Democratic candidate, Lewis Cass, for president. Lincoln rejoined by accusing the Democrats of doing likewise by sticking to the coattail of former Democratic president Andrew Jackson "like a horde of hungry ticks." He then utilized various comic images, ridiculing himself and Cass. Cass had served without great distinction as a general in the War of 1812:

By the way, Mister Speaker, did you know I am a military hero? Yes sir; in the days of the Black Hawk War, I fought, bled, and came away. Speaking of General Cass' career, reminds me of my own. I was not at Stillman's defeat, but I was about as near it, as Cass was to Hulls surrender; and, like him, I saw the place very soon afterwards. It is quite certain I did not break my sword, for I had none to break; but I bent a musket pretty badly on one occasion. If Cass broke his sword, the idea is,

he broke it in desperation; I bent the musket by accident. If
General Cass went in advance of me in picking huckleber-
ries, I guess I surpassed him in charges upon the wild onions.
If he saw any live, fighting Indians, it was more than I did; but
I had a good many bloody struggles with the mosquitos; and,
although I never fainted from loss of blood, I can truly say I
was often very hungry. Mr. Speaker, if I should ever conclude
to doff whatever our Democratic friends may suppose there is
of black cockade federalism about me, and thereupon, they
shall take me up as their candidate for the Presidency, I protest they shall not make fun of me, as they have of General
Cass, by attempting to write me into a military hero.

Finally he concluded his speech with a rejoinder to Democrats who had
claimed the Whigs were in disarray:

I have heard some things from New York; and if they are true,
one might well say of your party there, as a drunken fellow
once said when he heard the reading of an indictment for
hogstealing. The clerk read on till he got to and through the
words, "did steal, take, and carry away ten boars, ten sows,
ten shoats, and ten pigs," at which he exclaimed, "Well, by
golly, that is the most equally divided gang of hogs I ever

did hear of!" If there is any other gang of hogs more equally divided than the Democrats of New York are about this time, I have not heard of it.

As Lincoln's two-year stint in the House of Representatives drew to a close, he looked back on a rather unremarkable term. Although he had made an effort to speak out on issues of conscience such as slavery, attempted to serve his constituents faithfully, and toed the party line, he had no great accomplishments. His turn as Whig representative was up, and he could not seek reelection per the verbal agreements he had reached with other Springfield Whigs.

Before he left Washington, Lincoln had two achievements he could point to with some degree of satisfaction. On March 7, 1849, he was admitted to practice before the U.S. Supreme Court and argued a statute of limitations case in *William Lewis v. Thomas Lewis*. Three days later, he applied for a patent for a new and improved manner of combining adjustable buoyant chambers with steamboats or other vessels. Lincoln would be granted patent number 6,469 on May 22. He would be the only U.S. president to ever receive a patent.

Finally, Lincoln tried, unsuccessfully, to obtain a political appointment for the commission of the General Land Office in Illinois. He was offered, instead, the governorship of Oregon—a position he declined.

On March 4, 1849, Lincoln's term in Congress came to an end. He was forty years old, and it was time to return to Springfield—and his law practice.

LIFE ON THE CIRCUIT
1849-1854

L incoln's return to Springfield from his term in Congress on March 31, 1849, was not a triumphant one. While in the nation's capital, he had voted his conscience on issues such as the Mexican-American War and slavery, but his positions were not popular with most of his constituents. Since the Whigs' political arrangement prevented him from making another run for the House of Representatives and he did not want to go back to the state legislature, he decided to give up politics for a while and practice law "more assiduously than ever before."

Fortunately, his partner Billy Herndon had kept the law practice going and was glad to have Lincoln back. Lincoln and Herndon enjoyed an amicable business relationship, although neither were very good administrators. Their law office was the perfect model of chaos. In the middle was a large table, piled high with papers, including one bundle tied with a string that was labeled "When you can't find it anywhere else, look in this." There were a few old chairs scattered around, some bookshelves, an old battered secretary with pigeon holes for papers, the universal spittoon, and a decrepit old couch.

Evidently the piled papers weren't the important ones, because according to Herndon, Lincoln's plug hat was "his desk and his memorandum book." He always had the lining of his familiar, high hat stuffed with letters and notes. On at least one occasion, he had to apologize to a client for a tardy response to an important communication due to the seemingly incongruous reason he had "bought a new hat."

While relaxing in the law office, Lincoln loved to lie on the old couch and read newspapers out loud. As Lincoln put it: "I catch the idea by two senses, for when I read aloud I hear what is read and I see it; and hence two senses get it and I remember it better." Although this was annoying to Herndon, he was the junior law partner, so he didn't complain. The dingy old law office was truly a man's domain, and the fastidious Mary rarely, if ever, set foot in it, even though their home was only a few blocks away.

Tragedy struck the Lincoln home on February 1, 1850, when their second son, three-year-old Eddie, died of what was probably tuberculosis. Lincoln and Mary were heartbroken, and they composed a poem in his honor that was printed in a local paper.

Soon after Eddie died, Mary joined the First Presbyterian Church of Springfield. Lincoln did not become a member but attended occasionally with Mary and rented a family pew. Lincoln never formally joined any church because he disliked the many creeds and doctrines that they wanted their aspiring members to agree to. He said that "when any church will inscribe over its altar, as its sole qualification for membership, the Savior's condensed statement of the substance of both law and gospel, 'Thou shalt love the Lord thy God with all thy heart, and with all thy soul, and with all thy mind, and thy neighbor as thyself,' that church will I join with all my heart and all my soul." Nevertheless, Lincoln developed a close friendship with the pastor of the First Presbyterian Church, Reverend James Smith. Smith was just the sort of man Lincoln enjoyed talking to, an intellectual who had written a book with the rather capacious title of *The Christian's Defense, Containing a Fair Statement and Impartial Examination of the Leading Objections Urged by Infidels Against the Antiquity, Genuineness, Credibility, and Inspiration of the Holy Scriptures; Enriched with Copious Extracts from Learned Authors*.

A month or so after Eddie's passing, Lincoln and Mary were cheered by the news that she was expecting a third child.

Now that he was again focused on his law practice, Lincoln decided that a deeper study of mathematics would improve his ability to think logically and present more forceful arguments to juries. So he again added math books to his reading regimen and would later state proudly that he "nearly mastered" all six books of Euclid.

A return to the practice of law meant a return to the biannual trip around the Illinois Eighth Judicial Circuit. In the early 1850s, the Eighth Circuit included fourteen counties and involved a trek of more than four hundred miles that lasted eleven or twelve weeks. Most lawyers tried to minimize the time away from their families by either heading home Saturday in order to spend Sunday with them or dividing circuit duty with their partners. But Lincoln usually found an excuse to stay away from home on the weekends and did not split circuit work with Herndon. Judge Davis thought that this was because Lincoln "was not domestically happy."

Lincoln and Mary may have had problems in their marriage, but they maintained a deep commitment to one another and their children. Even though Lincoln's work took him away from home for several months out of the year, Mary was intensely proud of her husband's accomplishments in politics and the law.

Lincoln's life on the circuit followed a predictable routine. Judge Davis usually led the caravan of the state's attorney and twenty-five or thirty lawyers to town on Sunday or Monday. The lawyers took a day or two to communicate with clients and local counsel, prepare pleadings, and get ready for the opening of court midweek. Court sessions might last only a few days or as long as two weeks.

The circuit courts drew large crowds of spectators. In some county seats, such as Logan County's tiny Mount Pulaski, there was little in the way of established entertainment for the local populace besides the biannual drama of the circuit court. People seemed to enjoy the courtroom antics, even if it amounted to little more than watching a bunch of shrewd out-of-town lawyers arguing over the behavior of a neighbor's dog or the ownership of a litter of pigs.

An associate of Lincoln's, Henry C. Whitney, recalled:

> Our life on the Circuit was like a holiday. The semi-annual shopping of the country districts was transacted during Court week: the wits and county statesmen contributed their stock of pleasantry and philosophy; the local belles came in to see and be seen; and the Court House, from "early morn till dewy eve," and the tavern from dewy eve to early morn, were replete with bustle, business, energy, hilarity, novelty, irony, sarcasm, excitement, and eloquence. At the tavern the lawyers slept two in a bed and three or four beds were located in one room; at meals, the Judge, lawyers, suitors, jurors, witnesses, Court officers, and prisoners out on bail, all ate together and carried on a running conversation all along the dining-room. When Court was through, the Judge and lawyers would tumble into a farmer's wagon, or a carryall, or a succession of buggies, and trundle off across the prairie, to another court; stopping by the way at a farm-house for a chance dinner.

Even though circuit life was physically taxing, Lincoln reveled in it. The circuit riders would travel for hours at a time in their buggies or on horseback. The roads were often in terrible condition, and the weather on the Illinois prairie could be brutal. They ate what meals could be found, at farmhouses, taverns, and hotels. Evening entertainment usually consisted of meeting in the hotel parlor, telling jokes, and swapping stories. Of course, this was a pastime at which Lincoln excelled, and Judge Davis, who enjoyed Lincoln's sense of humor and the raucous fellowship more than anyone, became a close friend of Lincoln during these years.

Judge Davis liked to solicit Lincoln's humor not only in the hotel parlor but in the courtroom as well. Once, when the judge was making the first run through the docket, trying to dispose of such cases as could be handled quickly, he came across a long bill in chancery, drawn up by a talented but somewhat lazy lawyer. According to Whitney, Davis exclaimed, "'Why, brother Snap, how *did* you rake up energy enough to get up such a long bill?'

"'Dunno, Jedge,' replied Snap, squirming in his seat.

"The judge unfolded and held up the bill. 'Astonishing, ain't it? Brother Snap did it. Wonderful, eh! Lincoln?'

"Of course Lincoln was expected to heave a joke in at this point, and he was ready. 'It's like the lazy preacher,' Lincoln drawled, 'that used to write long sermons, and the explanation was, he got to writin', and was too lazy to stop.'"

Sometimes laziness has merit, like in the story Lincoln once related about a juror who was convinced a husband was wrong in bringing a lawsuit against his wife. In their deliberations, most of the jury was leaning toward the husband's side. The juror said, "Gentlemen, I am going to lie down to sleep and when you get ready to give a verdict for that woman, wake me up, for before I will give a verdict against her, I will be here until I rot and the [ants] carry me out of the keyhole."

Although Lincoln enjoyed the camaraderie of Judge Davis and other lawyers around the fireplace, he was not *always* sociable. With his melancholia, he preferred occasional solitude, and while the lawyers were laughing in the hotel parlor, he would slip away to some local entertainment in town such as a play at a local church or simply immerse himself in a book. It was not uncommon for Lincoln's friends to find him sitting quietly or talking to himself while staring at the flames in the fireplace, his mind a million miles away.

An example of his desire for privacy is recounted by Whitney:

> One evening, Lincoln was missing immediately after supper. He had no place to go, that we could think of—no friend to visit—no business to do—no client to attend to, and certainly no entertainment to go to. Hence: "Where is Lincoln?" was the question. I visited all the law offices and stores, but got no trace whatever; and at nine o'clock—an early hour for us—Davis and I went, grumblingly and hungry for mental food, to bed, leaving the problem unsolved. Now,

Lincoln had a furtive way of stealing in on one, unheard, unperceived, and unawares; and on this occasion, after we had lain for a short time; our door latch was noiselessly raised—the door opened, and the tall form of Abraham Lincoln glided in noiselessly.

"Why, Lincoln, where *have* you been?" exclaimed the Judge.

"I was in hopes you fellers would be asleep," replied he: "Well, I have been to a little show up at the Academy." He sat before the fire, and narrated all the sights of that most primitive of country shows, given chiefly to school children. Next night, he was missing again; the *show* was still in town, and he stole in as before, and entertained us with a description of new sights—a magic lantern, electrical machine, etc. I told him I had seen all these sights at school. "Yes," said he, sadly, "I now have an advantage over you in, for the first time in my life, seeing these things which are of course common to those, who had, what I did not, a chance at an education, when they were young."

Lincoln and Mary were blessed with a third son, William Wallace, who was born on December 21, 1850. Nicknamed Willie, he would later be acknowledged as the son that most closely resembled his father, due to his pleasant temperament and keen mind.

Lincoln's immediate family was growing, but he had little affiliation with his extended family. His parents lived in the eastern part of the state, nearly a hundred miles away, so he rarely saw them. Occasionally when circuit duties took him there, he would visit briefly, and Lincoln generously took care of them by paying the mortgage of their farm and deeding it back to them. But he still resented the way his father had treated him when he was young. In early January 1851, Lincoln's stepbrother, John D. Johnston, wrote to him that his father was dying and wanted to see him. Lincoln refused to go, saying that he was needed at home since Mary had recently had a baby and was sick. Instead, he wrote a gentle letter of condolence and told his father to "confide in, our great, and good, and merciful Maker." Thomas Lincoln died January 17, 1851.

By this stage of his legal career, Lincoln had become one of the most capable lawyers in the state. Leonard Swett, a skilled attorney who was on the circuit with Lincoln, said "any man who took Lincoln for a simple-minded man would very soon wake up with his back in a ditch." It is true that Lincoln did not have the legal knowledge that many of the other, more formally trained lawyers possessed. But according to his peer Isaac N. Arnold, Lincoln was "the strongest jury lawyer we ever had in Illinois." Lincoln was extremely effective in examining witnesses and brilliant at presenting evidence in a simple, logical manner that jurors could easily understand.

Robert Lincoln

Other lawyers on the Eighth Circuit agreed that as a jury lawyer, Lincoln had no equal. His droll ways and homely appearance quickly endeared him to jurors. He knew when to tell a funny anecdote that would make his legal argument more effective or render opposing counsel's less so. He also knew how to play upon the emotions of the jury, as illustrated when he pleaded the case of a Revolutionary War widow who had been cheated out of half her meager pension by an agent. Angered by the agent's actions, his personal notes on how he planned to plead the case to the jury were written as follows: "No contract. Not professional services. Unreasonable charge. Money retained by defendant—not given by plaintiff. Revolutionary War. Describe Valley Forge privations. Ice. Soldiers' bleeding feet. Plaintiff's husband. Soldier leaving home for army. Skin defendant. Close." The agent was sufficiently "skinned," and Lincoln won the case for the widow.

Leonard Swett faced Lincoln many times as opposing counsel. Once, during the process of jury selection, Lincoln began to ask the jurors whether or not they were acquainted with Swett's client. After two or three had answered in the affirmative, Judge Davis interrupted. "Now, Mr. Lincoln," he observed severely, "you are wasting time. The mere fact that a juror knows your opponent does not disqualify him."

"No, your Honor," responded Lincoln dryly. "But I am afraid some of the gentlemen may not know him, which would place me at a disadvantage."

In a Bloomington court, Lincoln was engaged in a case where the opposing attorney was a skilled young lawyer who was worried about being beaten. Finally the case went to the jury late at night. Worried, the young lawyer slept very little that night and, early next morning, learned that he had lost the case. Lincoln saw him "at the courthouse and asked him what had become of his case. With a downcast countenance, the young lawyer said, 'It's gone to hell.'

"'Oh well,' Lincoln responded. 'Then you'll see it again.'"

Lincoln was famous among his peers for offering his services to clients for a smaller fee than was customarily

Willie Lincoln

Tad Lincoln

charged. Many times, he returned money if he thought a client had paid him more than he deserved. Sometimes he would charge no fee at all.

An example of Lincoln's generosity was when he returned part of a fee he'd received from George P. Floyd of Quincy with the following note: "Dear Sir: I have just received yours of 16th, with check on Flagg & Savage for twenty-five dollars. You must think I am a high-priced man. You are too liberal with your money. Fifteen dollars is enough for the job. I send you a receipt for fifteen dollars, and return to you a ten-dollar bill."

This tendency to undercharge annoyed the other lawyers on the Eighth Circuit, and Judge Davis saw in it an opportunity to have some fun at Lincoln's expense. "Lincoln, you are impoverishing the bar by your picayune charges," Davis exclaimed. The judge, with the lawyers acting as jury, tried Lincoln for breach of decorum by what Davis called an "orgmathorical" (mock) court. Lincoln stood trial and, being found guilty, paid a small fine.

Another courtroom antic involved Lincoln's lawyer friend Ward Hill Lamon, who had ripped the seat of his pants and unmentionables in a wrestling match immediately before he had to go into a trial. While Lamon was pleading his case before the jury, his fellow lawyers noticed the rip and started chuckling among themselves. Soon they were passing a note down the line, pledging large sums of money toward the purchase of a new pair of pants for Lamon. When it reached Lincoln, he quietly glanced over the paper and then took up his pen to write after his name, "I can contribute nothing to the end in view."

Lincoln was not only a wit but usually quite imperturbable while facing opposing counsel in the courtroom. On one occasion, his opponent quoted a Latin maxim and then, either to impress his hearers or to embarrass Lincoln, added, "Is not that so, Mr. Lincoln?"

But Lincoln was not bothered by this barb. He responded dryly, "If that's Latin, I think you had better call another witness."

Lincoln was the master of using simple illustrations to make his point with juries. He defended a man who had been physically attacked by another man and had given his attacker a severe thrashing in self-defense. The attacker brought charges of assault and battery. Lincoln told the jury that his client was like a man who, in going along the highway with a pitchfork on his shoulder, was attacked by a fierce dog that ran out at him from a farmer's dooryard. In parrying off the brute with the fork, its prongs stuck into the dog and killed him.

"What made you kill my dog?" said the farmer.

"What made him try to bite me?"

"But why did you not go at him with the other end of the pitchfork?"

"Why did he not come after me with his other end?"

Lincoln whirled an imaginary dog about in his long arms and pushed its tail end toward the jury. With this demonstration, Lincoln not only got a guffaw from the jury but also won the case for his client.

Sometimes Lincoln took an indirect approach at attacking his opposing counsel's case. Once he defended a man in Bloomington against a charge of passing counterfeit money. A man named Stevenson who was present in the courtroom said that things were not going well for Lincoln's client during the trial, but when the chief witness for the people took the stand, he stated that his name was J. Parker Green. Stevenson said that Lincoln reverted to the chief witness's statement the moment he rose to cross-examine. He said Lincoln drawled in a suspicious, jesting way, "Why J. Parker Green? What did the J. stand for? John? Well, why didn't the witness call himself John P. Green? That was his name, wasn't it? Well, what was the reason he did not wish to be known by his right name? Did J. Parker Green have anything to conceal; and if not, why did J. Parker Green part his name in that way?"

Stevenson recalled that although "the whole examination was farcical," he thought "there was something irresistibly funny in the varying tones and inflections of Lincoln's voice as he rang the changes upon the man's name."

There was something in Lincoln's way of intoning his questions that made the jury suspicious of the witness. Stevenson admitted: "To this day I have never been able to rid my mind of the absurd impression that there was something not quite right about J. Parker Green."

The Lincolns' fourth son, Thomas, was born on April 4, 1853. Lincoln thought the baby as wriggly as a tadpole and henceforth he was known as Tad. Tad had a slight speech impediment that would cause him and his older brother Willie to become close over the years. Willie took it as his personal responsibility to help his younger brother communicate with others.

Lincoln had an increasing desire to help his wife with the children and spend more time at home. Thanks to the propagation of railway transportation in the mid-1850s, Lincoln's biannual travel on the circuit became easier. Because of this, he was able to come home on the weekends more frequently. This was indeed helpful to Mary, because her mood swings seemed to be increasing. She lost her temper more frequently and would often yell at her family. When this happened, Lincoln would tuck a book under his arm, put the boys in a wagon, and take them for a walk in order to give his wife a break.

One of their neighbors, Roland Diller, recalled one of Lincoln's outings with his sons, when he "was called to the door one day by the cries of children in the street, and there was Mr. Lincoln, striding by with two of his boys, both of whom were wailing aloud. 'Why, Mr. Lincoln, what's the matter with the boys?' I asked. 'Just what's the matter with the whole world,' Lincoln replied. 'I've got three walnuts, and each wants two.'"

Although he was trying to be more helpful with the children, like all husbands, Lincoln still found himself in occasional trouble with his wife. Once he and a friend, Judge Samuel Treat, had gotten involved in a game of chess at Lincoln's law office. Mary sent her oldest son to tell his pa that he should come home to supper. Robert soon returned home but without his father. After a little while, Robert was sent back to the law office, only to find Lincoln and the judge still absorbed in their game. Unable to get his father's attention, Robert gave the board a swift kick, scattering pieces everywhere. Unruffled, Lincoln stood up and calmly said, "Well, Jedge, I reckon we'll have to finish this game some other time."

While Lincoln put most of his time in the early 1850s into his law practice, he always kept apprised of what was going on in politics. He maintained correspondence with various political contacts, continued to make speeches, and maintained a prominent role in the Illinois political scene, even though he did not run for office.

For instance, in the summer of 1852, he made a political speech in support of Winfield Scott for president. In that address, he questioned Stephen A. Douglas's claim of confidence in providence. Lincoln said, "I suspect that *confidence* is not more firmly fixed with the Judge than it was with the old woman whose horse ran away with her in a buggy. She said she trusted in Providence till the britchen broke, and then she didn't know what on airth to do."

Speaking of providence, he might have continued in this vein—a successful prairie lawyer who occasionally dabbled in local politics—for the rest of his life, if it weren't for an event that took place on May 30, 1854. That event was the passage of the Kansas-Nebraska Act in the U.S. Congress, led by Senator Stephen A. Douglas in Washington, DC.

HAT IN THE RING
1854-1857

Even though Lincoln's law practice was quite successful and yielded a comfortable income, he was not completely satisfied with his life. He believed that as a lawyer he would never be able to accomplish anything of lasting significance, and he still desired to "be esteemed of [his] fellow men." It was about this time that Lincoln said to his partner William Herndon, "How hard, oh, how hard it is to die and leave one's country no better than if one had never lived for it!"

While Lincoln's stature as a lawyer in Illinois grew, he became increasingly involved in arguments before the Illinois Supreme Court, as well as in important civil cases representing corporate clients. He was more frequently employed by railroad companies such as the Illinois Central, and in one of his more important cases in early 1854, he pleaded a property taxes issue for that railroad. For this, he would receive his largest fee ever, $5,000, which he split evenly with Herndon.

Although Lincoln was doing more corporate legal work, he still employed his skills as a storyteller to influence juries. There was a case involving a plaintiff who brought suit against a man whose hogs had gotten through a fence and damaged his crops. The plaintiff seemed to have the upper hand. Appearing for the defendant, Lincoln conceded the damage to the crops and focused instead on the fence. According to Judge John M. Scott, Lincoln "told a little story about a fence that was so crooked that when a hog went through an opening in it, invariably it came out on the same side from whence it started. His description of the confused look of the hog after several times going through the fence and still finding itself on the same side was a humorous specimen of the best story telling. The effect was to make the plaintiff's case appear ridiculous and while Mr. Lincoln did not attempt to apply the story to the case, the jury seemed to think it had some kind of application to the fence in controversy—and shortly returned a verdict for the defendant."

In another case, a careless young lawyer who had patronized Lincoln during the trial felt the sting of the older lawyer's wit in rebuke. Lincoln likened his opponent to "an old mud scow that used to run on the Sangamon River," whose "engine was a rather weak affair and when they blew the whistle the wheels would stop." To the jurors, Lincoln said that his opponent "was in a somewhat similar condition, that when he was using his tongue so vigorously, his brain failed to work."

While Lincoln had lived the life of a prairie lawyer and small-time politician, Stephen A. Douglas, who was by then known as the Little

Giant, had risen to be one of the most powerful politicians in the U.S. Senate. Douglas was interested in building a transcontinental railroad from Chicago to the West Coast and would stop at nothing to attain his goal. Like most Democrats of that day, Douglas was not overly concerned about the spread of slavery into the new territories, so to enlist Southern senators' support for his railroad project, he proposed the passage of the Kansas-Nebraska Act, which would supersede the Missouri Compromise of 1820.

For more than thirty years, the Missouri Compromise had limited slavery, with the exception of the state of Missouri itself, to the territories below the latitude of Missouri's southern border. The Kansas-Nebraska Act eliminated the prohibition of slavery above that latitude. In place of the prohibition against slavery, Douglas substituted the doctrine of popular sovereignty, which allowed the residents of a territory to decide for themselves the status of slavery. Douglas had enough Democratic votes to push it through Congress in spite of unanimous Whig opposition, so on May 30, 1854, Democratic president Franklin Pierce signed the Kansas-Nebraska Act into law.

Douglas said that this act "would raise a hell of a storm." As it turns out, this was the understatement of the decade. Years later, he would recall that in 1854, he could have traveled "from Boston to Chicago by the light of [his] own [burning] effigy at night."

Although the North was outraged at the passage of the Kansas-Nebraska Act, the South rejoiced. The act became the hottest topic of the day, dominating the newspaper headlines and political discussion. It created an upheaval in the North's political landscape, effectively focusing the interest of various opposing political forces. These forces included a number of political groups, including Whigs, "Free-Soilers," and "anti-Nebraska" Democrats.

The popular protest against the Kansas-Nebraska Act precipitated a movement in the North to form a new antislavery "Republican" party that would fuse the Whigs, anti-Nebraska Democrats, and Free-Soilers into one. Although Lincoln was a Whig and reluctant to leave his old political party, like others, he began to recognize that the Whig Party was no longer strong enough to stand against the Democratic Party.

Lincoln said that he "had always hated slavery," but like the majority of Northerners, he had believed it would one day die a peaceful death. Although slavery had been prohibited from spreading further into the territories, it had remained strong in the Southern states over the previous thirty years. When Douglas's Kansas-Nebraska Act was signed into law, it breathed new life into slavery's future. If slavery was admitted in the western territories, it would mean new slave states. New slave states would increase political influence of the proslavery forces in Congress.

As a result of the Kansas-Nebraska Act, Lincoln began to believe that slavery would *never* die out. He feared it would not only spread into the new territories but may eventually return to Central and South America. As he rode the Eighth Circuit, he contemplated these possibilities and became increasingly alarmed—and frustrated—that he could do nothing about it on those lonely Illinois prairies.

Or could he? Although Douglas would not be up for reelection until 1858, the other Illinois Senate seat, currently held by pro-Nebraska Democrat James Shields, was up for grabs in 1854. Lincoln knew he had enough political capital in the Illinois Whig Party to receive strong support as their candidate for that office.

So in the summer of 1854, Lincoln began writing editorials and making speeches against the Kansas-Nebraska Act. His first truly important speech on this subject was in Peoria, Illinois, on October 16, 1854. Douglas had spoken that day to a large crowd about the act, extolling the positive points of popular sovereignty and saying repeatedly that he didn't care which way the people of the territories voted regarding slavery. Then, by previous agreement, Douglas let Lincoln take the podium to reply.

It is a testimony to Douglas's confidence in himself that he allowed Lincoln to speak to his audience. He had known Lincoln since their days in the legislature and the Eighth Judicial Circuit, and he said he regarded Lincoln "as the most difficult and dangerous opponent I have ever met." In Lincoln's three-hour-long response to Douglas, he presented many of the major themes he would use over the coming years in his continued attacks on slavery.

In Peoria, Lincoln used the Declaration of Independence as his springboard for attacking the moral injustice of slavery. He said, "no man is good

Abraham Lincoln

enough to govern another man, without that other's consent. I say this is the leading principle—the sheet anchor of American republicanism…When the white man governs himself that is self-government; but when he…also governs another man, that is more than self-government—that is despotism. If the negro is a man, why then my ancient faith teaches me that 'all men are created equal'; and that there can be no moral right in connection with one man's making a slave of another." He called for the American people to "re-adopt the Declaration of Independence, and with it, the practices, and policy, which harmonize with it."

He attacked Douglas's statements that he "didn't care one way or the other whether slavery was voted up or voted down" in the new territories. He said that Douglas's indifference demonstrated a lack of moral principle and that he was at odds with the spirit of the Declaration of Independence. In contrast to Douglas, Lincoln declared that he hated slavery: "I hate it because of the monstrous injustice of slavery itself. I hate it because it deprives our republican example of its just influence in the world—enables the enemies of free institutions, with plausibility, to taunt us as hypocrites."

Lincoln angered Douglas when he stated that it was former Democratic presidential candidate Lewis Cass who was the real author of popular sovereignty, not Douglas. Douglas boomed out his response: "No, Sir! I will tell you what was the origin of the Nebraska bill. It was this, Sir! God created man, and placed before him both good and evil, and left him free to choose for himself. That was the origin of the Nebraska bill!"

Lincoln, who "looked the picture of good nature and patience," smilingly replied, "I think it is a great honor to Judge Douglas that he was the first man to discover that fact." This elicited a laugh from the audience—and a scowl from the Little Giant.

An issue that Lincoln had to handle carefully in both the Peoria debate and in many others with Douglas was the common prejudice toward black people by white people. Illinois was one of the worst Northern states in this regard, as evidenced by its previous passage, in 1848, of a bill that outlawed the settlement of free black people within its borders. Illinois was the only free state to ever do this.

Douglas and other Democrats took advantage of this prejudice effectively during the three-month-long campaign and claimed that Lincoln stood not only for equal political treatment of black people, but that he was also an abolitionist at heart who wanted complete equality between the races. This included social standing, voting, opportunities for employment, intermarriage, and many other things that were absolute anathema to most whites of that day.

In his speeches and letters, Lincoln tried to avoid alienating any of the various anti-Kansas-Nebraska Act groups in the state. He still considered himself a Whig and was cautious about aligning himself too closely with the newest of the anti-Nebraska forces, the Republican Party.

In a letter to his old friend Joshua Speed, Lincoln wrote:

> I think I am a Whig; but others say there are no Whigs, and that I am an abolitionist...I am not a Know-Nothing. That is certain. How could I be? How can anyone who abhors the oppression of negroes, be in favor of degrading classes of white people? Our progress in degeneracy appears to me to be pretty rapid. As a nation, we began by declaring that "all men are created equal." We now practically read it "all men are created equal, except negroes." When the Know-Nothings get control, it will read "all men are created equal, except negroes, and foreigners, and Catholics." When it comes to this I should prefer emigrating to some country where they make no pretense of loving liberty—to Russia, for instance, where despotism can be taken pure, and without the base alloy of hypocrisy.

In Lincoln's day, U.S. senators were chosen by the state legislatures rather than direct vote of the people. When the legislature began balloting for senator in early February of 1855, Lincoln had the most support among the Whigs, but it was not enough to give him a majority. In the end, he had to withdraw from the contest and throw his support to another of the candidates, anti-Nebraska Democrat Lyman Trumbull. As a result of this, Trumbull was elected senator on February 8, 1855. Although disappointed in the result, Lincoln took his defeat philosophically and consoled himself with pledges of support from Trumbull and other anti-Nebraska politicians for Lincoln's anticipated race against Douglas, who would run for reelection to the Senate in 1858.

Stephen A. Douglas

After his unsuccessful bid for the Senate as a Whig in 1855, over a year would pass before Lincoln would decide that his political future required him to switch from the Whig to the Republican Party. In late May of 1856, Lincoln met with a group of anti-Nebraska editors in Decatur and urged moderation on the slavery issue in order to promote unity among anti-Nebraska forces in Illinois. He was afraid that a radical antislavery program would cause the loss of many supporters in the central and southern part of the state. Toasted as "our next candidate for the U.S. Senate," Lincoln thanked them and hinted he wasn't ready to make a speech, saying that he was very much in the position of a man attacked by a robber who demanded his money. "I have no money," said the victim, "but if you will go with me to the light, I will give you my note." The audience laughed, but Lincoln was still obliged to speak.

Lincoln spoke at Decatur for half an hour. He said in jest that he "was a sort of interloper there and was reminded of the incident of an ugly man who, while riding on horseback through the woods, met an equestrienne. He reined his horse to one side of the bridle path and stopped, waiting for the woman to pass. She also checked her horse to a stop and looked him over in a curious sort of a way, and finally broke out with, 'Well, for land sake, you are the homeliest man I ever saw.'

"'Yes, madam, but I can't help it,' the man rejoined.

"'No, I suppose not,' she said, 'but you might stay at home.'"

Lincoln said, "that he felt as though he might have stayed at home on that occasion."

Lincoln finally concluded that the new Republican Party would be able to assemble sufficient strength from the anti-Nebraska forces in Illinois to effectively combat the Democratic Party, so he joined the Republicans. On May 29, 1856, Lincoln delivered the keynote address at the Republican rally that met in Bloomington for the purpose of adopting a party platform. John L. Scripps, editor of the Chicago *Democratic Press*, a Republican paper, was present for the speech. Incredibly, no reliable or verifiable accounts of what Lincoln said that evening survive today, and it is now known as Lincoln's "lost speech." Scripps recalled the impact of Lincoln's speech later: "Never was an audience more completely electrified by human eloquence. Again and again during its delivery they sprang to their feet and upon the benches and testified by long-continued shouts and the waving of hats how deeply the speaker Lincoln had wrought upon their minds and hearts. It fused the mass of hitherto incongruous elements into perfect homogeneity."

Two weeks after Lincoln's speech in Bloomington, the first Republican National Convention met in Philadelphia on June 17–19. They nominated John C. Fremont, a famous western explorer, as the first Republican candidate for president of the United States. The Illinois delegation there tried to have Lincoln selected as the vice-presidential candidate, and he received 110 votes before being dropped on the second ballot. On hearing this surprising news from the Philadelphia convention, Lincoln said, "I reckon that ain't me; there's another great man in Massachusetts named Lincoln, and I reckon it's him."

Whereas northern Illinois was safely Republican and expected to go for Fremont in the national election, southern Illinois was likely to vote for Democratic presidential candidate James Buchanan. Lincoln threw himself into campaigning for the Republican ticket, delivering more than fifty speeches, mostly in the central part of the state where the outcome was up for grabs.

On November 4, the nation went to the polls. Even though Buchanan won all of Illinois's Electoral College votes for president and the presidential election too, Republicans in the Prairie State were nevertheless encouraged. Their candidate, William Bissell, had won the governorship, and they had established their new party as a powerful force in Illinois. Lincoln himself had risen significantly in political stature in Illinois and throughout the Midwest. He was increasingly in demand for political speeches at Republican gatherings in neighboring states.

On December 10, 1856, at a Republican banquet in the Tremont House Hotel in Chicago, Lincoln mocked the Democrats' prediction that the Republican candidate for governor, William Bissell, could never be elected. Lincoln said that their conduct brought to mind the man in a cave who, when a bear had put its head into the hole and shut out all the daylight, called to his friend outside, "What was darkening the hole?"

"Ah," cried the friend, who was holding on to the animal's tail. "If de tail breaks, you'll find out!"

While her husband was on one of his political trips in 1856, Mary had a second story added to their house. When Lincoln returned, he pretended not to recognize his home, asking his neighbor, "Wilkie can you tell me where old Abe Lincoln lived around these parts?" Surprised by what she had done, Lincoln said to his wife, "Mary, you remind me of the story of the fellow who went to California and left one baby at home and when he returned three years later, found three. The fellow looked at his wife and then at the children and said, 'Well, Lizzie, for a little woman and without help, you have raised thunder amazingly.'"

Lincoln had become much more involved in the raising of his two younger sons than he had been with his two older boys. It was probably the death of his son Eddie years before that significantly impacted Lincoln's attitude toward parenting. Regretting his long absences from home, which had kept him from a close relationship with his oldest son Robert, Lincoln sought as much time with Willie and Tad as possible when he was home. He also wanted his sons to be "unrestrained by parental tyranny" and made very little effort to discipline them.

Herndon found this lack of discipline quite annoying on the Sunday mornings that Lincoln brought the boys to the law office. Herndon recalled that "the boys were absolutely unrestrained in their amusement. If they pulled down all the books from the shelves, bent the points of all the pens, overturned inkstands, scattered law-papers over the floor, or threw the pencils into the spittoon, it never disturbed the serenity of their father's good-nature." While Lincoln indifferently relaxed on the couch and read newspapers, Herndon said that the "little urchins" would pile papers and books in the middle of the floor and literally dance on them, and he wanted to "wring their little necks." Out of respect to the senior partner, he bit his tongue and "kept [his] mouth shut."

In March 1857, the Supreme Court tossed a bombshell into the North's antislavery movement. Chief Justice Roger Taney, in the infamous *Dred Scott* decision, ruled that black people could not be citizens of the United States and Congress had no power to prohibit slavery in any territory. He also expressed his opinion that slaves and descendants of slaves "had no rights which the white man was bound to respect." This was an attack on the antislavery cause and a direct challenge to the new Republican Party. The *Dred Scott* decision outraged many in the North and inspired people like Lincoln to greater resolve in their fight against slavery.

In May 1857, Lincoln made an important speech in Springfield that condemned the *Dred Scott* decision. Although he did not go so far as to encourage resistance to the Supreme Court's ruling, he did say that the Republicans should do their best to have it reversed. Lincoln attacked Taney's assertion that black people were not included in the Declaration of Independence's promise of equality. He argued, however, that the Declaration's authors "did not intend to declare all men equal in all respects. They did not mean to say all were equal in color, size, intellect, moral development, or social capacity," but they "did consider all men created equal—equal in 'certain inalienable rights, among which are life, liberty, and the pursuit of happiness.'"

Although the majority of Lincoln's time was devoted to his law practice for the remainder of the year, he continued to lay the groundwork for his race against Senator Douglas in 1858. He wrote letters, made occasional speeches, strategized with anti-Nebraska men, and promoted his political agenda in every way he could while he traveled the circuit. Herndon said that "he was always calculating, and always planning ahead. His ambition was a little engine that knew no rest."

BEST STUMP SPEAKER IN THE WEST
1857-1861

O ver the course of the fall and winter of 1857–58, the issue of slavery in the Kansas territory exploded in the nation's newspaper headlines. Proslavery forces drafted a state constitution, known as the Lecompton Constitution, which allowed slavery in Kansas. The document was sent to Congress without first being submitted for full referendum by the people of the Kansas territory. Antislavery forces in the territory, who composed the vast majority of the population, were outraged that they were not allowed to vote.[1]

Stephen A. Douglas was angry too. He had assured the nation that popular sovereignty would allow the *majority* of the people of a territory to decide the fate of slavery. When Democratic President Buchanan decided to ignore the majority's wishes and urge Congress to admit Kansas to the Union as a slave state, Douglas openly defied the president, causing a huge rift in the

---

1. For Lecompton Constitution and referendum, see McPherson, *Battle Cry of Freedom*, 162–66.

Democratic Party. This defiance pleased abolitionists in the East, who began hinting that Illinois Republicans should support Douglas's reelection bid.

But Illinois Republicans were not about to support the despised Douglas, thinking they finally had a chance to defeat him. So Republican delegates to the Illinois state convention on June 16, 1858, passed a resolution declaring that "Abraham Lincoln is the first and only choice of the Republicans of Illinois for the United States Senate, as the successor of Stephen A. Douglas." Lincoln's second bid for the U.S. Senate, this time as a Republican, had finally begun.

Lincoln delivered a carefully prepared address to the convention, which introduced several themes that he would repeat over the coming weeks. He began with a Biblical admonition:

> A house divided against itself cannot stand. I believe this government cannot endure, permanently half slave and half free. I do not expect the Union to be dissolved—I do not expect the house to fall—but I do expect it will cease to be divided. It will become all one thing, or all the other. Either the opponents of slavery, will arrest the further spread of it, and place it where the public mind shall rest in the belief that it is in course of ultimate extinction; or its advocates will push it forward, till it shall become alike lawful in all the States, old as well as new—North as well as South.

On July 9, 1858, Douglas presented the opening speech of his Senate campaign at Chicago's popular Tremont House Hotel. In his typical, forceful way, Douglas attacked Lincoln's speech and declaimed that it advocated "a war of the North against the South." Knowing the prejudices of his audience, he claimed that Lincoln was advocating racial equality, and that "this government of ours is founded on the white basis...It was made by the white man, for the benefit of the white man, to be administered by white men."

Lincoln was in the audience during Douglas's speech, and the following evening at the Tremont House, he presented his reply. He continued with this tactic, listening to Douglas's speeches and then replying the following evening. Lincoln challenged Douglas to formal debate, and finally the Democratic senator reluctantly agreed to seven debates over the course of the next two months. The debates were to be held at Ottawa, Freeport, Jonesboro, Charleston, Galesburg, Quincy, and Alton.

Prior to Douglas's return to Illinois for the Senate campaign, supporters in Washington had expressed their confidence that he would easily defeat the unknown Lincoln. But Douglas knew Lincoln well and said to them, "I shall have my hands full. He is the strong man of his party—full of wit, facts, dates, and the best stump-speaker, with his droll ways and dry jokes, in the West. He is as honest as he is shrewd; and if I beat him, my victory will be hardly won."

In the following weeks, Lincoln and Douglas crisscrossed the state, traveling via rail to nearly two hundred independent speaking engagements. Douglas enjoyed free passage in a private railroad car, provided by his friend, the vice president of the Illinois Central Railroad, George B. McClellan. Douglas was also allowed to bring along his wife and an army of supporters, reporters, and admirers. Lincoln, on the other hand, frequently traveled alone, sometimes as a passenger on the very same trains Douglas and his supporters were on.

On his way to an appointment in southern Illinois, Lincoln and a few friends were traveling in the caboose of a freight train. The freight train suddenly switched off the main track to allow a special train to pass. In that special train, Douglas and his entourage were being conveyed to the same town. The passing train was decorated with banners and flags and carried a band that was playing "Hail to the Chief." As the train whistled past, Lincoln broke out in a fit of laughter and said, "Boys, the gentleman in that car evidently smelt no royalty in our carriage."

Although the candidates spoke independently more than two hundred times at various locations and venues in Illinois, it was the seven Lincoln-Douglas debates that gained the most national attention. Newspaper reporters from all over the country attended, taking notes and writing articles on what each candidate said. The press was extremely partisan, with both Democratic and Republican organs exaggerating the reaction of the audience or the impact of their favorite candidate's argument on his opponent. As a result of the newspaper coverage, Lincoln would become, like

Douglas, a national political figure. "The prairies are on fire!" headlined one eastern newspaper.

The crowds numbered in the thousands at each debate, all of which had a carnival-like atmosphere. The audiences were entertained by fireworks, brass bands, glee clubs, and booming cannons. Political signs and bunting hung everywhere. The debate structure was arranged with the first candidate having one hour to make his opening argument, followed by an hour and a half rebuttal from the second candidate, and then a final half hour for rejoinder by the first candidate. Paid stenographers kept notes.

The debaters were a study in contrast. The Little Giant was only five feet four inches in height but was of stocky build, well groomed, and had a bold, aggressive platform presence. He had a deep, booming voice and was a natural debater. Lincoln was six feet four inches tall, lanky, carelessly dressed, less comfortable in front of an audience, and had a higher-pitched voice.

Despite his apparent advantages, Douglas had a tremendous respect for Lincoln's skills as a debater. He once said about Lincoln, "Every one of his stories seems like a whack across my back…Nothing else—not any of his arguments or any of his replies to my questions—disturbs me. But when he begins to tell a story, I feel that I am to be overmatched."

Lincoln also had great respect for Douglas. He said of Douglas, "It is impossible to get the advantage of him. Even if he is worsted, he so bears himself that the people are bewildered and uncertain as to who has the better of it."

The contestants stood on an open platform, usually without notes, and spoke as loudly as they could. The primary subject of the debates was slavery, especially the expansion of slavery into the new territories. With some variation, the speeches they delivered over the course of the seven debates had standard themes. Lincoln denounced slavery as a moral evil, called for a return to the ideals of equality expressed in the Declaration of Independence, and attacked Douglas's indifference to slavery in the new territories as, in reality, a thinly veiled desire to support its spread. Douglas called Lincoln's House Divided speech inflammatory, constantly accused him and the "Black Republican Party" as proponents of complete racial equality, and defended his popular sovereignty idea as a paradigm of democratic principle.

Douglas routinely demeaned black people and had a powerful, combative manner of presentation. Lincoln was usually nervous and awkward when he began his speech, until he warmed to his subject. Then his well-honed logic, his jury skills of simplifying complicated questions, and his homely stories would take effect, helping him to drive home his points forcefully. As his speech progressed, he commanded increasing respect and interest from the audience.

The first debate took place on August 21, 1858, in Ottawa, which was in the northern part of the state. In his rejoinder to Douglas, Lincoln said, "There is no reason in the world why the negro is not entitled to all the natural rights enumerated in the Declaration of Independence, the right to life, liberty, and the pursuit of happiness." In that same speech, Lincoln made reference to a Biblical verse, Genesis 3:19, which he would continue to use in future speeches when arguing for the black man's rights. He said that the black man had "the right to eat the bread, without leave of anybody else, which his own hand earns," and in that, "he is my equal and the equal of Judge Douglas, and the equal of every living man."

Lincoln did not use as much humor in the debates as was expected, admitting later that he thought the occasion was "too grave and serious" for a lot of jesting. At Ottawa, however, he couldn't resist digging at Douglas when he responded to a disingenuous compliment Douglas had paid him. He said, "As the Judge had complimented me with these pleasant titles, (I must confess to my weakness,) I was a little 'taken,' for it came from a great man. I was not very much accustomed to flattery and it came the sweeter to me. I was rather like the Hoosier, with the gingerbread, when he said he loved it better than any man, and got less of it [than any man]."

At the second debate in Freeport, Lincoln drew a laugh from the audience when he said that "the Judge is a great man, while I am only a small man." But he then went on the offensive and asked Douglas several questions, one of which would, ultimately, destroy the Little Giant's chances of ever winning the White House. With the *Dred Scott* decision in mind, Lincoln asked Douglas whether or not the residents of a territory could in any lawful way, against the wishes of any citizen of the United States, exclude slavery from their limits prior to the formation of a state constitution.

With this question, Lincoln laid an ominous trap for Douglas. If Douglas said no, then he was violating his own popular sovereignty principle. If he said yes, he risked alienating the South, whose leaders wanted a president who would guarantee their right to take slaves into the new territories. Douglas hoped to one day be president, but he decided to stick to his popular sovereignty principles and answered yes. His affirmative answer, hereafter known as the Freeport Doctrine, would eventually cause a split in the Democratic Party and crush Douglas's chances of becoming president in 1860.

Douglas was not above lying, especially when he knew that his lie could not be disproved on the spot. This exasperated the scrupulously honest Lincoln, as is shown by Lincoln's response to Douglas in the next debate at Jonesboro on September 15. After listening to Douglas deliver an often-repeated lie, Lincoln said, "I do not know how to deal with this persistent insisting on a story that I know to be utterly without truth. It used to be a fashion amongst men that when a charge was made some sort of proof was brought forward to establish it, and if no proof was found to exist, the charge was dropped. I don't know how to meet this kind of an argument. I don't want to have a fight with Judge Douglas, and I have no way of making an argument up into the consistency of a corn-cob and stopping his mouth with it."

At the debate in Charleston on September 18, Lincoln denounced Douglas's unsubstantiated attack on one of Lincoln's political points by saying, "You remember that by a course of reasoning Euclid proves that all the angles in a triangle are equal to two right angles. Euclid has shown you how to work it out. Now, if you undertake to disprove that proposition, and to show that it is erroneous, would you prove it to be false by calling Euclid a liar?"

At the fifth debate, held in Galesburg on October 7, the speakers stood on a platform that adjoined one of Knox College's classroom buildings. To reach the platform, the speakers had to walk through the building and climb through a window. When climbing out, Lincoln quipped "at last I have been through college."

At Galesburg, Lincoln said, in referring to a document previously forged by Democrat Thomas Harris in his race for Congress, "[This] fraud having been apparently successful upon that occasion, both Harris and Douglas have more than once been attempting to put it to new uses, as the woman said when her husband's body was brought home [with the pockets] full of eels. When asked what should be done with him, she said 'take the eels out and set him again'; and so Harris and Douglas have shown a disposition to take the eels out of that stale fraud by which they got the first election, and set that fraud again more than once."

At the debate in Quincy on October 13, Lincoln joked, "To keep up that humbug about popular sovereignty he [Douglas] has at last invented this sort of do-nothing sovereignty of the people excluding slavery by doing nothing at all. I ask you is this not running down his popular sovereignty doctrine to death, till it has got as thin as the homeopathic soup that was made by boiling the shadow of a pigeon that was starved to death?"

At the last debate in Alton on October 15, Douglas was physically exhausted and his voice weakened from a cold—but Lincoln was the picture of health and confidence. In making his final statement of the debates, Lincoln closed eloquently with a brief synopsis of "the real issue" of the differences between himself and Douglas and between Republicans and Democrats of the day. In it, he said that he and the Republican Party looked upon slavery as being a "moral, social, and political wrong," and that the Democrats did not. "It is the eternal struggle between these two principles—right and wrong—throughout the world. They are the two principles that have stood face to face from the beginning of time; and will ever continue to struggle. The one is the common right of humanity and the other the divine right of kings. It is the same principle in whatever shape it develops itself. It is the same spirit that says, 'You work and toil and earn bread, and I'll eat it.'"

At last, the debates were over, and the people went to the polls in November. Lincoln won the popular vote in Illinois by nearly four thousand votes but lost the vote for senator in the legislature by 46 to 54. He probably would have won if the state legislature representation was not misallocated, which gave Douglas an unfair advantage.

After the loss, Lincoln good-naturedly told a journalist that "he felt like the Kentucky boy, who, after having his finger squeezed pretty badly, felt 'too big to cry, and too badly hurt to laugh.'" Actually, Lincoln was bitterly disappointed in the outcome, but he put the best face on the loss he could and called it "a slip and not a fall." He wrote to a friend, "I am glad I made the late race. It gave me a hearing on the great and durable question of the age, which I could have had in no other way; and though I now sink out of view, and shall be forgotten, I believe I have made some marks which will tell for the cause of civil liberty long after I am gone."

But Lincoln was far from gone in the political scene. He was now a national figure, the unknown Republican who had stood toe to toe with the most powerful Democratic leader in America. Lincoln, who would later say, "if slavery is not wrong, nothing is wrong," had gained a reputation as a moderate who resolutely stood against the expansion of slavery. Horace Greeley of the *New-York Tribune* said of Lincoln:

> The man who stumps a State with Stephen A. Douglas, and meets him, day after day, before the people, has got to be no fool. Many a man will make a better first speech than Douglas, but, giving and taking, back and forward, he is very sharp…I don't believe we have got another man living who would have fought through that campaign so effectively and at the same time so good-naturedly as he did…Lincoln went through with perfect good nature and entire suavity, and beat Stephen A. Douglas.

Lincoln had become the spokesman not only for the Illinois Republican Party, but for all anti-Nebraska forces that wanted to keep slavery confined to the existing slave states. Invitations to speak at political engagements poured in, but Lincoln turned most of them down. He needed to go back to work, telling one, "I am absolutely without money now for even household purposes."

Although he had to return to the courtroom, Lincoln nevertheless displayed an unconquered spirit when he said, with determination, "The fight must go on. The cause of civil liberty must not be surrendered at the end of one, or even one hundred, defeats."

Lincoln had worked on and off at his law practice during the Senate race but had relatively few high-paying cases in 1858. Even the case that would become his most celebrated, in the spring of 1858, he did as an act of charity. Lincoln used an almanac to prove that the witness claiming to have seen his old friend Jack Armstrong's son Duff kill another man by the light of a full moon was lying. The moon was not high enough in the sky that night to provide sufficient light.

In 1859, Lincoln represented Melissa Goings, a seventy-year-old woman accused of murdering her seventy-seven-year-old husband by hitting him over the head with a stick of firewood. She pleaded self-defense at the trial, and evidently fled the courthouse after a short conference with her attorney. When court bailiff Robert Cassell charged that Lincoln had suggested she flee, he replied, "I didn't run her off. She wanted to know where she could get a good drink of water, and I told her there was mighty good water in Tennessee." Goings eventually turned up in California.

Lincoln helped another elderly client at a trial in Chicago, where he was involved in the indictment of a young U.S. army officer for an assault on the aged gentleman. Lincoln opened the case by saying, "This is an indictment against a soldier for assaulting an old man."

Conscious of his superior rank, the officer indignantly interrupted by saying, "Sir, I am no soldier, I am an officer!"

"I beg your pardon," said Lincoln, grinning blandly; "then gentlemen of the jury, this is an indictment against an officer, who is no soldier, for assaulting an old man."

During another trial, Lincoln ridiculed the long-winded ways of competing counsel, who had just delivered an elaborate address to the jury and at one point went into great detail about habits of storks in Holland. Lincoln remarked to a fellow lawyer, "That beats me! Blackwell can concentrate more words into the fewest ideas of any man I ever knew."

Although Lincoln was focused on his law practice, he still maintained a vigorous political correspondence. One Illinois editor told Lincoln that he wanted to endorse him for president of the United States, but Lincoln replied, "I do not think myself fit for the Presidency." Lincoln realized his star was rising, but he also knew party leaders such as New York senator William H.

Seward and Governor Salmon P. Chase of Ohio were seeking the Republican nomination, and they had much greater national reputations. Nevertheless, Lincoln's "little engine" kept working away, and in 1859, he spoke at party rallies in Ohio, Indiana, Iowa, Kansas, and Wisconsin, repeating many of the same themes he had in his debates with Douglas. In February 1860, the *Chicago Tribune* endorsed Lincoln for president.

That same month, Lincoln made his first trip to New England. Ostensibly this trip was to visit his oldest son Robert, who was attending Phillips Exeter Academy in preparation for Harvard Law School. Lincoln had told Robert, when his son was contemplating the decision to pursue law at the prestigious university, "If you do, you should learn more than I ever did, but you will never have so good a time."

But Lincoln had more than one reason to travel to the East. Some New York Republicans had invited him to speak at the famous abolitionist preacher Henry Ward Beecher's church (the venue was later switched to the Cooper Union in New York City). Knowing that many important people would be there, Lincoln prepared an address on the subject of the Founding Fathers' policy on slavery. Hoping to make a good impression, he even bought a new black suit for the occasion.

But his first impression on the audience at Cooper Union, which included many influential Republicans and newspapermen, was not a favorable one. He had forgotten to remove a pencil stuck above his ear, his suit had been wrinkled badly in transit, and he looked quite disheveled sitting next to the immaculately dressed Beecher on stage. When he began his speech, his high-pitched midwestern drawl and salutation of "Mister Cheerman" caused many of the sophisticated listeners to shift uncomfortably in their seats.

But, typical of Lincoln, as his speech progressed, he warmed to his subject and became absorbed in his argument. The audience soon lost interest in his rough appearance and focused on what he was saying. He expounded upon the Founders' positions on slavery and their desire to see it die out. He spoke of the detestableness of slavery on moral grounds. He attacked the Supreme Court's *Dred Scott* decision. Facts and figures to support his position rolled quickly from his tongue. He presented a convincing, logical argument about the Founders' hope for the demise of slavery, and his only nod toward humor was in a barb aimed at the Southern slave owners: "You will not abide the election of a Republican President! In the supposed event you will, you say, destroy the Union; and then, you say, the great crime of having destroyed it will be upon us! That is cool. A highwayman holds a pistol to my ear, and mutters through his teeth, 'Stand and deliver, or I shall kill you, and then you will be a murderer!'"

He closed his speech with the following declamation: "Neither let us be slandered from our duty by false accusations against us, nor frightened from it by menaces of destruction to the Government nor of dungeons to ourselves. Let us have faith that *right makes might*, and in that faith, let us, to the end, dare to do our duty as we understand it!"

The audience, having become almost hypnotized by his presentation, suddenly leaped to their feet and burst into spontaneous cheers and applause.

The eastern Republican newspapers reprinted his speech and heaped praise upon Lincoln. Suddenly the unrefined prairie lawyer was in demand everywhere, and he made several other speeches throughout New England before heading home. He returned to Illinois with an enhanced national reputation and would soon admit that the idea of running for president was a taste "that is in my mouth a little."

After his Cooper Union speech, a friend pointed out to Lincoln that he had forgotten to remove the pencil he had stuck above his ear. Lincoln said that his absentmindedness on that occasion made him think of the story of an old Englishman "who was so absentminded that when he went to bed he put his clothes carefully into the bed and threw himself over the back of his chair."

Lincoln's correspondence with eastern politicians and newspapermen increased significantly. In letters and subsequent speeches in the Midwest, he pointed out that the Democrats—supposed heirs of the political party of Thomas Jefferson, author of the Declaration of Independence—now considered liberty to be more about the slaveholders' right to own slaves than about all men being "created equal." In a letter to Boston Republicans, he wrote, "I remember once being much amused at seeing two partially intoxicated men engage in a fight with their great-coats on, which fight, after a long, and rather harmless contest, ended in each having fought himself out of his own coat, and into that of the other. If the two leading parties of this day are really identical with the two in the days of [Thomas] Jefferson and [John] Adams, they have performed about the same feat as the two drunken men."

The Democratic Party held its 1860 presidential convention in Charleston, South Carolina, beginning on April 23. In their assembly, the delegates found it impossible to come up with a presidential candidate who appealed to both the northern and southern wings of the party. Douglas was the most likely choice, but his Freeport Doctrine, which he had expressed in his debates with Lincoln, eliminated his chances of accumulating sufficient southern support. Southern Democrats wanted a candidate who was more reliable on the slavery question, and after fifty-seven futile ballots, the northern Democrats packed their bags and went home.

A few weeks later, at the Illinois Republican state convention, the delegates selected "Lincoln the Railsplitter" as their choice for presidential candidate. Even though the Republican National Convention was to be held May 15–18 in nearby Chicago, Lincoln did not attend. It was not considered "decorum" for the candidates themselves to attend the national political conventions, so to lead the floor fight for his nomination in Chicago, Lincoln selected his old circuit friend Judge Davis to head the efforts of Illinois's twenty-two delegates.

Recognizing that he would not be the first choice for most of the delegates, Lincoln instructed his team to allow the other states' delegates to vote for their favorite candidates on the first ballot but to try to build increasing strength with the second and subsequent rounds of votes. He telegraphed Judge Davis, "I authorize no bargains," and waited in Springfield for results.

William H. Seward, the Republican front-runner from New York, sent to Chicago his wily political manager Thurlow Weed, along with his state's seventy delegates and thirteen railroad cars full of support-ers. Although Seward had the advantage of being the front-runner, he had a radical antislavery reputation and was not universally popular with Republicans.

The night before the convention, Judge Davis and his team began can-vassing with the delegates from Vermont, Indiana, Pennsylvania, and New Jersey. Candidates from these states knew that their men—such as Simon Cameron from Pennsylvania—would not have enough support to win the nomination. So the Lincoln team told the candidates that, if they could not have their favorite, they could at least stop Seward. Pennsylvania had fifty votes to offer, and when the delegation from the Keystone State asked for a cabinet post for their candidate, Davis paused. Reminded of Lincoln's directive to make no binding deals, Davis cracked, "Lincoln ain't here," and complied with Pennsylvania's request.

On the first ballot, Seward fell sixty votes short of victory. Lincoln was second, followed by Cameron, Chase, and the others. The Lincoln team strategy kicked in on the second ballot when the votes from Pennsylvania and other states switched to the Railsplitter. At the end of the second ballot, Lincoln had pulled within three votes of Seward, and the others were far behind.[2]

Lincoln had the momentum, and on ballot three, the prairie lawyer of Illinois won the Republican nomination for president of the United States. Celebrations in Springfield began as soon as the telegraph announced the news, with cheering and backslapping all around. Lincoln received dozens of hearty congratulations, including a telegraph message from delegate N. M. Knapp that said simply, "We did it. Glory to God." Thinking of Mary, Lincoln left the celebration early by saying he wanted to go tell a "lady over yonder" the election results.

On June 18, the Democratic Party convened their second presidential convention, this time in Baltimore, to see if they could finally come to agreement on a presidential nominee. After various floor fights and a walkout by some of the delegates, the convention selected Douglas as the Democratic nominee. But Douglas, thanks to the Freeport Doctrine, was unacceptable to the slaveholders. Consequently, Southern delegates left the convention and later held a "stump" convention, selecting Vice President John C. Breckinridge of Kentucky as their "proslavery" candidate. This split the Democratic Party and greatly increased Lincoln's chances for victory. The entry of a fourth candidate, John Bell of Tennessee, further diluted the Southern vote.[3]

---

2. For events at the 1860 Republican Convention, see Donald, *Lincoln*, 246–51.
3. For a cogent analysis of the 1860 presidential race, see McPherson, *Battle Cry of Freedom*, 213–33.

OUR PORTRAIT GALLERY.—No. 5.

THE SPLIT-TAIL DEMOCRACY.

OLD ABE.—*Here's a rail specimen of the Split-tail Democracy,*
DOUGLAS.—*"We are all Democrats."*
BRECKINRIDGE.—*"So we are."*

For " The Rail Splitter."

RAIL LYRICS.—No. 5.

The deed is done, their day is o'er,
Two possums fought at Baltimore;
Now let them scratch, and let them wall,
Old Abra'm has them " *in a rail.*"

Well let them fight, and let them bite,
And quarrel for the bone ;
The maxim says, at such a time—
" The honest get their own."   T. RAIL, Esq.

From *The Chicago Rail Splitter*, Abraham Lincoln's Campaign Newsletter, July 21, 1860. Abraham Lincoln—the original "rail-splitter"—is shown using a split rail to trap the two Democratic candidates, Douglas and Breckinridge, in the presidential election of 1860.

During the presidential race, a mountain of mail poured in to Lincoln in Springfield. He hired the efficient, unemotional young German immigrant John Nicolay and the tactful, Ivy League–educated John Hay to sift through it. Somehow, in the flood of letters, one written by an eleven-year-old girl named Grace Bedell, of Westfield, New York, came to Lincoln's attention. The little girl offered the presidential candidate some advice. She inquired about his family, expressed her admiration, and told the clean-shaven candidate that his face was too thin so he should grow whiskers. She justified this by saying, "All the ladies like whiskers and they would tease their husbands to vote for you and then you would be President."

Lincoln not only read the letter but answered it: "My dear little Miss. Your very agreeable letter of the 15th is received. I regret the necessity of saying I have no daughters. I have three sons—one seventeen, one nine, and one seven, years of age. They, with their mother, constitute my whole family. As to the whiskers, having never worn any, do you not think people would call it a silly affection [sic] if I were to begin it now? Your very sincere well wisher, A. Lincoln." In spite of this whimsical reply, Lincoln must have agreed with Miss Bedell, because by the time he left for Washington, he would be sprouting a beard.

Despite the fact his name wasn't printed on most southern ballots, Lincoln "the Railsplitter" was elected president of the United States on November 6, 1860. Hannibal Hamlin of Maine became vice president. Gifts and letters of congratulation poured in to Springfield, including a new stovepipe hat from a New York hatmaker. As he tried it on, Lincoln said, "It fits me perfectly. Well, wife, if nothing else comes of this scrape, we are going to have some new clothes, are we not?" That, of course, was something Mary was counting on.

In the weeks after the election, Lincoln used the governor's room in the state house in Springfield to meet with visitors, prospective cabinet members, office seekers, and various political leaders. Not wanting to inflame the South further, he refused to make policy statements, and maintained that all he had to say on slavery and its spread into the new territories "had already been said." When one visitor asked him to disclaim all intention of interference with slavery in the South, Lincoln referenced Luke, chapter 16, of the Bible to emphasize his point: "If they hear not Moses or the prophets, neither will they be persuaded though one rose from the dead."

Lincoln did not think it was right to continuously make statements to appease the South, and he illustrated this with a story about his youngest sons. Willie had a toy that Tad wanted, and when Willie refused to give it up, the younger boy made such a fuss about it, Lincoln asked the older brother to let his sibling have the toy in order to keep him quiet. "No, sir," Willie responded. "I must have it to quiet myself."

In the early weeks after he won the election, Lincoln didn't believe that the crisis would sustain momentum. Having been born in Kentucky and living among people who had southern roots, he was confident he "knew" the southern people.

Lincoln certainly knew the working-class man of the South, but he had never rubbed elbows with the likes of "fire-eaters" such as William Lowndes Yancey, Robert Barnwell Rhett, or Louis Trezevant Wigfall. These men, as members of the South's aristocracy, were wealthy, powerful, arrogant, and firm believers in a class society that placed slaves at the very bottom. Afraid of losing their privileged status, they had advocated Southern independence at any cost. Speaking of his fellow secessionists, Yancey said, "We shall fire the Southern heart—instruct the Southern mind—give courage to each other, and at the proper moment, by one organized, concerted action…precipitate the cotton states into a revolution."

Lincoln believed that the pro-Union leaders of the South would ultimately prevail over the planter class and help the South come to its senses before it went so far as to declare independence. But while Lincoln waited in Springfield, the nation's fate was in the hands of the inept James Buchanan. Buchanan made little effort to dissuade the South from calling conventions, preparing for war, and voting to secede from the Union. Consequently, conventions for secession began with South Carolina on December 20, 1860, and continued over the following weeks with Mississippi, Florida, and Alabama. Eventually, seven states would vote to secede before Lincoln took office.

In the meantime, in Springfield, Lincoln corresponded with friends from all over the country, urging Republicans to stand firm against the South's demands for the spread of slavery into the new territories. "Let there be no compromise on the question of extending slavery," he wrote Senator Lyman Trumbull in early December. "If there be, all our labor is lost, and, ere long, must be done again." In speaking of his frustration with the South's political leaders on their insistence of states' rights over federal rights, Lincoln observed that the advocates of that theory always reminded him of "the fellow who contended that the proper place for the big kettle was inside of the little one."

In order to prepare for the worst, Lincoln appointed some of the strongest men he could to his cabinet. William H. Seward, the former governor of New York whom Lincoln had defeated for the Republican presidential nomination, was chosen for secretary of state. Salmon P. Chase, former governor of Ohio, who also lost the nomination to Lincoln, was selected for the Treasury Department. Pennsylvanian Simon Cameron, whom Lincoln was forced to accept because of the deal Judge Davis made at the convention, became secretary of war.

The weeks passed, and Lincoln's departure for Washington finally drew near. Shortly before he left, Lincoln went to pay his respects to his elderly stepmother in eastern Illinois. With tears, she anxiously told him that she was afraid his enemies would assassinate him in Washington and that she would never "be permitted to see him again." Lincoln tried to reassure her that he would be safe. He tenderly responded, "No, no Mama, they will not do that. Trust in the Lord and all will be well, and we will see each other again."

The day before leaving for Washington, Lincoln made a last trip to his law office to visit his junior partner, Billy Herndon, and talk over old times. He told Herndon to leave the sign "Lincoln and Herndon" hanging outside. "Give our clients to understand that the election of a President makes no change…If I live I'm coming back some time, and then we'll go right on practicing law as if nothing had ever happened." Before he left, he expressed his resolve to deal with the looming crisis when he told Herndon, "I am decided; my course is fixed; my path is blazed. The Union and the Constitution shall be preserved and the laws enforced at every and at all hazards. I expect the people to sustain me. They have never yet forsaken any true man."

On February 7, 1861, the seven states of the Deep South went through with their threat and adopted a provisional constitution, declaring themselves a new nation—the Confederate States of America. They selected the former senator from Mississippi, Jefferson Davis, as their president, and Lincoln's old congressional associate Alexander H. Stephens of Georgia as vice president. Lincoln finally realized that his confidence in the South had been misplaced, and he would have to deal more firmly with it than he had hoped.

On February 11, standing on the rear platform of the train in Springfield that was to take him to Washington, he looked at the crowd of well-wishers and, holding back tears, offered this impromptu farewell:

My friends—No one, not in my situation, can appreciate my feeling of sadness at this parting. To this place, and the kindness of these people, I owe everything. Here I have lived a quarter of a century, and have passed from a young to an old man. Here my children have been born, and one is buried. I now leave, not knowing when, or whether ever, I may return, with a task before me greater than that which rested upon Washington. Without the assistance of that Divine Being, who ever attended him, I cannot succeed. With that assistance I cannot fail. Trusting in Him, who can go with me, and remain with you and be everywhere for good, let us confidently hope that all will yet be well. To His care commending you, as I hope in your prayers you will commend me, I bid you an affectionate farewell.

The train pulled out of the station.

PUTTING THE FOOT DOWN
1861

Lincoln's circuitous train trip to Washington took nearly two weeks, and he made numerous stops along the way so people could see their new president-elect. On February 11, 1861, in Thorntown, Indiana, Lincoln expressed his frustration over the slowness of his trip with a funny story. He said there once "was a man who had hired a horse to take him to a political convention, where he was to receive his party's nomination for office. The horse was so slow, however, that when the man finally arrived, he found his opponent nominated and the convention adjourned. When returning the horse, he said to the stableman, 'This is a fine animal of yours—a fine animal.'

"'Do you think so?'

"'Certainly, but never sell him to an undertaker.'

"'Undertaker! Why not?'

"'Because if the horse were hitched to a hearse, resurrection day would come before he reached the cemetery.'

"'So,' Lincoln said, 'if my journey goes on at this slow rate it will be resurrection day before I reach the capital.'"

When the train stopped at Westfield, New York, Lincoln called for little eleven-year-old Grace Bedell, the girl who had suggested he grow whiskers. Years later Grace recalled, "He climbed down and sat down with me on the edge of the station platform. 'Gracie,' he said, 'look at my whiskers. I have been growing them for you.' Then he kissed me. I never saw him again.'"

At Leaman Place, Pennsylvania, his presence on the train platform was not enough to appease the boisterous crowd, who kept calling for Mrs. Lincoln. He finally brought her out and, while she stood beside him, joked that this was "the long and the short of it."

As the rebellion rhetoric in the South continued to spread, Lincoln found it necessary to say more about the looming crisis. He assured audiences that he would not accept disunion, that he would protect federal property, and that he would enforce the laws. In a speech to the New Jersey legislature on February 21, he affirmed his devotion to peace but added that "it may be necessary to put the foot down firmly."

In Philadelphia, on the morning of February 22, Lincoln was warned by detective Allen Pinkerton that the "plug-uglies" of Baltimore had hatched a plan to assassinate him when he changed trains in their city the next day. This was corroborated by other sources at the time, and in the interest of avoiding a fight between troops and civilians, Lincoln heeded Pinkerton's advice and deviated from the planned schedule by taking the night train from Philadelphia to Washington. Newspapers claimed he had "snuck in" to Washington overnight, some claiming he wore a Scottish plaid cap and long military cloak and others adding a kilt to the disguise.

Finally, on March 4, Inauguration Day arrived. General-in-Chief Winfield Scott, the old hero of the War of 1812 and the Mexican-American War, wanted to be certain that the inauguration ceremonies occurred without any interference from the Southern sympathizers in town. So the parade route for the presidential entourage and the Capitol grounds were heavily guarded.

Lincoln's inaugural speech was primarily addressed to the Southern people and intended to both clarify his policies and reach out to them in what he hoped would be a conciliatory tone. In the address, he said that he believed the South had no legal right to secede, and he intended to "hold, occupy, and possess the property and places belonging to the government." By property, he meant the remaining forts that the South had not yet confiscated, such as Fort Sumter in the middle of Charleston Harbor. He assured Southerners that "the government will not assail you. You can have no conflict, without being yourselves the aggressors." Hoping to avoid war, Lincoln closed with the plea that "we are not enemies, but friends. We must not be enemies."

After the inauguration, Lincoln shook hands in the White House receiving line for several hours, a task that he later said was harder work than splitting rails. That evening, he received a message from Fort Sumter's commander, Major Robert Anderson. This was the same officer who as a lieutenant had mustered Lincoln into the army during the Black Hawk War thirty years before. Anderson warned the new president that he and his small garrison would be forced to surrender Fort Sumter unless he was soon resupplied.

Fort Sumter had become an important symbol to both sides. To the North, it was a sign of the Union, and to the South, a representation of unwelcome federal authority. Confederate general Pierre Gustave Toutant Beauregard had surrounded Fort Sumter with dozens of cannon and prepared to attack if Lincoln did not order Major Anderson, Beauregard's old artillery instructor at West Point, to surrender.

Lincoln wanted to avoid starting a war over Sumter, but he did not want to surrender the fort either. He settled on a plan whereby he would send word to the governor of South Carolina that Sumter would be resupplied with food but not reinforced, unless the provisioning ship was fired upon. In that case, he would land ammunition and additional troops on Sumter. Lincoln reckoned that if Jefferson Davis allowed the provisioning ship in, he would be able to bloodlessly fulfill his promise to "hold and occupy" federal property. If, on the other hand, Davis fired on the ship bringing provisions, he would not only be firing the first shot of the war—he would be "firing on bread."

On March 29, Lincoln presented this plan to his cabinet, and everyone except Seward agreed. Satisfied with this support, Lincoln ordered ships to sail from New York to Charleston Harbor to carry out his plan.

Seward objected to the plan and tried to change Lincoln's mind with a letter on April 1. He suggested that he, as secretary of state, should make these sorts of decisions, not the president. Lincoln read the letter and politely rejected this idea. Seward, put in his place, never challenged Lincoln's authority again. He and Lincoln, who had similar personalities and both enjoyed telling funny stories, would soon become good friends. Seward would later confide to his wife that "the president is the best of us."

On April 6, Lincoln sent word to the governor of South Carolina to inform him that food and provisions were being sent to the Union soldiers at Fort Sumter and that no reinforcement of the fort would be attempted unless the provisioning ship was fired upon. Davis was quickly advised of this and decided to attack Sumter before the supplies could reach them. At 4:30 a.m., April 12, the war began when Confederate cannon started firing on Fort Sumter. The bombardment lasted thirty-four hours before Major Anderson was compelled to surrender.

On April 15, Lincoln issued a proclamation calling for seventy-five thousand volunteers to put down the rebellion in the seceded states. He also called for Congress, which was not in session, to meet in special assembly on July 4. In the meantime, as commander in chief, he directed the nation's war efforts by what would later be known as executive order.

While the South rejoiced over Davis's attack on Fort Sumter, the North was outraged. Well over seventy-five thousand Northern men tried to enlist, and thousands were turned away after the quota had been reached.

While the North had been incensed by the attack on Fort Sumter, the South became infuriated at Lincoln's call for troops. The states of the upper

South, including Virginia, Arkansas, Tennessee, and North Carolina, responded by joining the Confederacy—which now included eleven states. The border slave states of Kentucky, Missouri, Delaware, and Maryland remained, at least for the time being, in the Union. Thousands of Southern men rushed to enlist in the army, and men on both sides feared that the war would be over before they could fight.

Washington had very few troops protecting it, and the fact that it was surrounded on three sides by Maryland—which had not committed to support of the Union—and one side by hostile Virginia was alarming to government officials. On April 19, Union reinforcements, including the Sixth Massachusetts Regiment and units from Pennsylvania, were assaulted in Baltimore by a pro-Southern mob. The governor of Maryland demanded that Lincoln send no more troops across Maryland soil, but the president refused. "I must have troops," Lincoln stated to a delegation from the governor. "Our men are not moles, and can't dig under the earth; they are not birds, and can't fly through the air. There is no way but to march across, and that they must do."

The South began rapidly assembling armies and taking over federal property such as the Gosport Navy Yard in Norfolk, Virginia. Lincoln decided he must quickly take decisive action in order to protect Washington from a possible attack by Confederate forces.

When it came to the authority of the president during time of rebellion, Lincoln was on uncharted ground. The Constitution was vague as to the responsibilities of each branch of government during war, and the fact that this was an armed rebellion made things even more unclear. Since Congress was not in session, Lincoln planned to make executive decisions to deal with the crisis and later submit his actions to Congress for approval or disapproval when they assembled on July 4. These decisions dealt with exigencies such as the need to suspend the writ of habeas corpus, the increase in size of the regular army, and the proclamation of a blockade of Southern ports.

Opposition to Union troop movements continued in Maryland, with telegraph lines being cut and railroad bridges burned by Confederate sympathizers. Lincoln had once quipped that Maryland must be a good state to move *from*, and these acts of sabotage must have reinforced this opinion. On April 27, Lincoln authorized the suspension of the writ of habeas corpus along the railroad lines from Washington to Philadelphia. This allowed local military commanders to temporarily jail anyone they suspected of trying to impede progress of the troops being sent to Washington. Maryland farmer John Merryman was imprisoned at Fort McHenry in Baltimore Harbor for burning several bridges, and he petitioned Supreme Court Justice Roger Taney for a writ of habeas corpus. On May 26, Taney issued the writ, and instead of complying, Lincoln ignored Taney's ruling and kept Merryman imprisoned.[1]

---

1. For Lincoln's reaction to Taney's ruling on Merryman, see White, *Abraham Lincoln and Treason*, 1.

Some members of the Democratic Party were adamantly opposed to the war and protested that Lincoln did not have the authority to suspend the writ. Lincoln, in his response, pointed out that pro-Confederate forces were violating laws and putting the nation's capital in danger of capture and asked the logical question—were "all the laws, but one [habeas corpus] to go unexecuted, and the government itself go to pieces lest that one be violated?"

Although Lincoln was now president of the United States, he was still a devoted father. According to sixteen-year-old Julia Taft, if there was any motto or slogan of the White House during the early years of the Lincolns' occupancy, it was "Let the children have a good time." Julia was the older sister of the two Taft boys, Bud and Holly, whom Mary had asked to come to the White House to be playmates for Willie and Tad. Sons of patent office examiner Horatio Nelson Taft, they were close to the Lincoln boys in age and equally full of mischief. Julia was given the unenviable task of semiofficial babysitter.

Julia described eleven-year-old Willie as the "most lovable" boy she ever knew. He was "bright, sensible, sweet-tempered, and gentle-mannered." Seven-year-old Tad she said had "a quick fiery temper, very affectionate when he chose, but implacable in his dislikes." She had a favorable impression of Mary, who "was so pleasant and kind to me." Lincoln frightened her, in spite of his kindly disposition, simply because he was president. He never quite broke her of the habit of standing up every time he walked into the room.

But she slowly warmed up to Lincoln, who called her "Jewly" and nick-named her "Flibbertigibbet." When she asked him what a flibbertigibbet was, he playfully said, "it's a small, slim thing with curls and a white dress and a blue sash who flies instead of walking."

The Taft and Lincoln boys quickly became inseparable, and Julia had many challenges in her assignment to make sure "those young rascals don't tear down the White House." She had to contend with pet goats, dogs, make-believe circuses, jackknives in church, imaginary ships on the White House roof, and four boys who loved to barge in on the president's import-ant meetings.

An example of Julia's trials was the day Tad threw a ball and broke a large mirror in the White House vestibule where the Marine Band played at receptions. The boys and Julia were soon standing around the broken pieces "in speechless horror." Tad indifferently kicked a piece of glass and observed that Pa wouldn't care, but Willie said, "It is not Pa's looking glass. It belongs to the United States Government." The children quickly told him that he had to throw salt over his left shoulder and say the Lord's Prayer backward if he wanted to avoid seven years of bad luck. He was in the process of looking for his father's Bible to help with the prayer when someone told them that their goat Nanko had escaped. They forgot the mirror and searched for Nanko until they finally corralled him in one of the gardener's flower beds.

Although the Lincoln boys were focused on having a good time, their father had to concentrate on the national crisis. In the first few evenings of July, while everyone else's eyes turned skyward toward the Great Comet of 1861, Lincoln's eyes were focused on putting the finishing touches to one of the most important speeches of his life. This would be his address to the special session of Congress on July 4, where he would justify the extraordinary measures he had taken to preserve the Union. In the pinnacle of that speech he said:

> This issue embraces more than the fate of these United States. It presents to the whole family of man, the question, whether a constitutional republic, or a democracy—a government of the people, by the same people—can, or cannot, maintain its territorial integrity, against its own domestic foes. It presents the question, whether discontented individuals, too few in numbers to control administration according to organic law, in any case, can...break up their Government, and thus practically put an end to free government upon the earth.

Congress agreed with Lincoln and formally approved nearly all of his executive decisions.[2] Secretary of State Seward would later say that, although the bold actions taken by the president early in the war "could have brought them all to the scaffold," they were the most crucial decisions of Lincoln's entire presidency.

Besides building up sufficient military forces for the war, Lincoln's immediate problem in facing the South was to keep the border states of Maryland, Kentucky, and Missouri from joining the Confederacy. The governments and people of these slave states were divided in their loyalties, and Lincoln knew that he had to be careful to keep from provoking them into rebellion.

Maryland surrounded Washington, DC, on three sides, so Lincoln had to be the most aggressive there. In order to quickly eliminate any chance that Maryland would secede, he used military force to arrest those members of the Maryland state government who were pro-secession.

In Missouri, he had to walk cautiously at first, since the governor was openly pro-Southern. St. Louis was a hotbed of Southern activity, and on May 11, one Union regiment, the 5th Missouri of the U.S. Reserve Corps, was attacked by a mob shortly after the men were mustered into the army.

---

2. For details on Congress's approval of Lincoln's decisions, see White, *Abraham Lincoln and Treason*, 143n19.

But as Union military strength increased in the state, Lincoln was able to secure St. Louis and expand Union influence.

Kentucky, which had formally declared neutrality, was the most delicate problem. The governor was pro-Southern but the legislature pro-Northern. Lincoln realized that it was essential he avoid any military violation of the state's neutrality and refused to allow his military commanders to cross the Kentucky border.

As if problems with the border state governments were not enough, in May, Union general Benjamin F. Butler complicated things politically for Lincoln when he started accepting runaway slaves within his lines at Fort Monroe, Virginia. He declared them "contraband of war" and refused to return them to their former masters. Even though this was technically illegal, Lincoln did not reverse this policy. Congress soon solved the legality issue when, on August 6, it passed the First Confiscation Act, which provided that slaves previously used by the Confederacy for military purposes could be confiscated from their owners.

About this time, Lincoln was discussing legality issues with British correspondent Edward Dicey, and the subject of Southern statesmen's pretensions of legality in their internal government came up. Lincoln said these statesmen reminded him "of a hotel-keeper down at St. Louis who boasted that he never had a death in his hotel…for whenever a guest was dying in his house he carried him out to die in the street."

One of the presidential duties Lincoln enjoyed was visiting the army in order to review the troops and bolster morale. On one occasion, Lincoln was approached by a junior officer who had encountered some trouble with his brigade commander, William Tecumseh Sherman. The young officer was quite angry and said, "Mr. President, I have a cause of grievance. This morning I went to General Sherman and he threatened to shoot me."

"Threatened to shoot you?" asked Lincoln. "Well, (in a stage whisper) if I were you I would keep away from him; if he threatens to shoot, I would not trust him, for I believe he would do it."

To another soldier, who had complained about a minor issue, Lincoln said, "Now, my man, go away, go away! I cannot meddle in your case. I could as easily bail out the Potomac River with a teaspoon as attend to all the details of the army."

On another visit to the army, when Lincoln was being conveyed around camp in a mule-drawn wagon, the soldier driving the wagon swore so profusely at his animals that it captured the president's attention. Lincoln said to the soldier, "Excuse me, are you Episcopalian?" Surprised, the soldier said no, he was a Methodist. "Well," said Lincoln, "I thought you must be an Episcopalian, because you swear just like Governor Seward, who is a churchwarden."

While Lincoln was building up the army and keeping order in the border states, the eastern press and various members of Congress began pressuring him to invade Virginia. Horace Greeley, editor of the powerful *New-York Tribune*, emblazoned the paper's masthead with "On to Richmond!" and other eastern papers soon joined in the clamor for military action. Lincoln knew he must heed public opinion, and since many of the soldiers had enlisted for only ninety days, he decided to order his army to attack.

But who was to lead the invasion? General Scott was too old and fat to take field command, so regular army officer Brigadier General Irvin McDowell was ordered to take the North's force of thirty-five thousand green troops southward. On July 21, McDowell fought a Confederate army under command of General Beauregard at Manassas, Virginia. Initially, the Union forces pushed the Confederates back, but Confederate general Thomas Jonathan Jackson's brigade refused to retreat and earned their commander the nickname "Stonewall." Confederate reinforcements under command of General Joseph E. Johnston arrived toward the end of the day, and the Union army was defeated. During their retreat, the North's green troops lost all semblance of organization en route to Washington and were reduced to an unorganized mass by the time they arrived there. But the Confederates, in victory, were nearly as disorganized as their foe and failed to follow up their battlefield success with an attack on the capital.

The defeat at Manassas, or Bull Run as it was called in the North, was demoralizing to the army, but it also had some positive benefits for the Union. The "On to Richmond!" crowd was silenced, and the North realized that it would take much more than a few thousand troops and a couple of months' effort to defeat the South. Lincoln signed a bill authorizing enlistment of half a million three-year volunteers.

Recognizing his own ignorance of modern warfare, Lincoln acquired books on military strategy from the Library of Congress, among which was *Elements of Military Art and Science* by Henry W. Halleck. He realized that General McDowell had lost the confidence of the public and had to be replaced. The most obvious choice of command was a general named George B. McClellan, who had won some minor military engagements in western Virginia and had skillfully manipulated the press to exaggerate their importance. McClellan had been the vice president of the powerful Illinois Central Railroad back in the days when Lincoln was that company's attorney, so the president had some familiarity with him. When the Washington newspapers and many congressmen began clamoring for his instatement to command, Lincoln ordered McClellan to take charge of the army around Washington. But he was not completely convinced of McClellan's ability, so Lincoln made him subordinate to General Scott.

General McClellan was an excellent organizer and confidently took charge of the disorderly mass of men he inherited from General McDowell on July 26. He dubbed it "the Army of the Potomac" and industriously went to work equipping, training, and organizing the men. He soon gained the confidence of the army, the president, the cabinet, and most of the political leaders in Washington. His men affectionately called him "Little Mac" and enthusiastically cheered him during the many parades and reviews he held for visiting dignitaries.

Although things were beginning to look promising in the eastern theater, events in Missouri were presenting problems for Lincoln. In early August, the Union lost the battle of Wilson's Creek in the south-central part of the state, and the Union commander in Missouri, General John C. Fremont, overreacted. On his own authority, Fremont, who had been the first Republican nominee for president in 1856, decided to impose martial law in Missouri as well as order the emancipation of the state's disloyal residents' slaves.

Although Fremont's actions delighted Republican radicals, it caused great anxiety to Unionists in Kentucky. Lincoln told one U.S. senator, "I think to lose Kentucky is nearly…to lose the whole game," and ordered Fremont to countermand his emancipation order. When Fremont refused, Lincoln overruled him and relieved him of command.

Lincoln's quick action kept Kentucky in the Union but caused a tremendous outcry of disapproval among the abolitionists of the North. Nevertheless, it was the right decision for the moment, and Union sentiment continued to increase in the border states—especially Kentucky.

In early September, Jefferson Davis concluded that the strongest military positions for the South's defense of Tennessee were geographically located in Kentucky, and he ordered an army across the border to Columbus. This violation of Kentucky's neutrality tipped public opinion in the Bluegrass State against the Confederacy. In response, Kentucky's pro-Northern legislature requested that Union troops be sent into the state, and the majority of residents switched their allegiance to the Union.

On November 8, another policy crisis was thrust upon Lincoln by a subordinate commander, and this one had international implications. A U.S. Navy warship, the USS *San Jacinto*, commanded by Captain Charles Wilkes, stopped the RMS *Trent* in the Atlantic Ocean and seized two Confederate diplomats, James M. Mason and John Slidell. Mason and Slidell were on their way to London and Paris to seek recognition of the Confederacy as a separate nation and hoped to also arrange military aid for the South. Captain Wilkes was hailed as a hero in the North and was praised by the press, members of Congress, and members of Lincoln's cabinet.

The British government protested that the seizure of the diplomats was illegal and Britain's neutrality had been violated. Britain prepared to send troops to Canada for possible battle with Union forces if the diplomats were not allowed to continue their journey. When Lincoln told his cabinet of his reluctance to go to war with Britain over the incident, only one cabinet member agreed with him.

This reminded Lincoln of a drunken man in Illinois who happened to stray into a church while a revival meeting was in progress. He walked up the aisle to the very front pew, joined audibly in the singing, and said "Amen" at the close of the prayers. After a while, he became drowsy and fell asleep. Before the meeting closed, the pastor asked the usual question, "Who are on the Lord's side?" and the congregation arose en masse. When he asked, "Who are on the side of the Devil?" the congregation sat down.

About that time, the sleeper woke up, and, seeing the minister on his feet, arose. Looking around, the drunken man said, "I don't exactly understand the question, but I'll stand by you, parson, to the last. But it seems to me that we're in a hopeless minority."

In spite of being in the minority, Lincoln told his cabinet "one war at a time," and ordered the Confederate diplomats' release. Great Britain backed down from its threat to send troops, and the crisis subsided.

The *Trent* affair's peaceful resolution reminded Lincoln of an incident that occurred in his youth. He recalled that "thar were two fields behind our house separated by a fence. In each field was a big bulldog, and those dogs spent the whole day racing up and down, snarling at each other through the fence. One day they both came at the same moment to a hole big enough for either of 'em to get through." So, Lincoln said, "Well, gentlemen, what do you think they did? They just turned tail and scampered away as fast as they could in opposite directions. Now, England and America are like those bulldogs."

At the end of the *Trent* crisis, Lincoln responded to a visitor's praise of Great Britain by telling a story: "It makes me think of an Indian chief that we had out West. He was visited by an Englishman once who tried to impress him with the greatness of England. 'Why,' said he to the Chief, 'the sun never sets on England.' 'Humph!' said the Chief. 'Probably because God wouldn't trust 'em in the dark.'"

Although major crises such as the *Trent* affair and Fort Sumter consumed a great deal of Lincoln's attention, the biggest consumer of the president's time in 1861 was the never-ending line of office seekers and visitors. Lincoln's secretaries, Nicolay and Hay, did their best to shield the president, as well as put some sort of limitations on the hours he received visitors, but Lincoln himself would break the rules as soon as they were made, saying, "They don't want much, and they don't get but little, and I must see them."

Several hours a week, Lincoln held what he called his "public opinion baths." Virtually anyone who wanted to talk to the president was allowed a five-minute audience. Citizens with petty grievances, office seekers, soldiers, soldiers' wives, businessmen, or people who just wanted to shake his hand could line up in the hallway and wait for their turn to meet the commander in chief. Lincoln said his constant conversations with visitors and handing out of patronage jobs to office seekers in the midst of civil war reminded him of the man who was so busy in letting rooms at one end of the house that he couldn't put out the fire that was burning in the other.

Some of the more well-connected office seekers sent members of Congress or government officials to petition the president for them. When a commissioner to the Hawaiian Islands was to be appointed, eight applicants filed their papers. The ninth applicant sent a delegation, who told Lincoln that not only was their man fit for the office, but he was also in bad health, and a residence in that balmy climate would be of great benefit to him. Before they had gotten far with their plea, Lincoln retorted,

"Gentlemen, I am sorry to say that there are eight other applicants for that place, and they are all 'sicker'n your man.'"

The busy president generally tried to let his cabinet members run their own departments without interference. The only major exception to this rule was the War Department, because Lincoln had lost all confidence in the secretary of war, Simon Cameron. Cameron, whose nickname was "the Great Winnebago Chieftain," had been forced on Lincoln by Judge Davis's deal with the Pennsylvania delegates at the Republican convention in Chicago. The criticisms leveled at Cameron ranged all the way from negligence to incompetence and corruption. Chairman of the House Ways and Means Committee Thaddeus Stevens told Lincoln that Cameron was a thief but "I don't think that he would steal a red hot stove." When Cameron demanded Stevens retract this statement, Stevens complied by telling Lincoln, "I believe I told you he would not steal a red hot stove. I now take that back."

Although he watched Cameron closely, Lincoln usually let Salmon P. Chase run the Treasury Department without interference, even though he knew that the treasury secretary was using patronage appointments to build political opposition against him. Chase had resented Lincoln's receiving of the Republican nomination, and in 1861, he began working to increase his chances of replacing Lincoln on the Republican ticket in 1864. Lincoln acknowledged his treasury secretary's subterfuge and would later say that "I suppose he will, like the bluebottle fly, lay his eggs in every rotten spot he can find."

GULLIVER ABE, IN THE WHITE HOUSE, ATTACKED BY THE LILLIPUTIAN OFFICE-SEEKERS.

From *Frank Leslie's Budget of Fun*, March 15, 1861. Lincoln's well-known problems with the constant pestering of office seekers was captured on the front page of this popular weekly magazine.

Secretary Chase came up with the first "greenback" dollar bill to be issued by the U.S. Treasury. Of course he decided that his portrait, rather than Lincoln's, should appear on it. After the greenback idea had been accepted, Lincoln's cabinet discussed the advisability of putting on the paper dollar a legend similar to the "In God We Trust" that was being considered for new coins. When they asked Lincoln his opinion, he replied, "If you are going to put a legend on the greenback, I would suggest that of Peter and John, 'Silver and gold have I none, but such as I have give I thee.'"

While Lincoln was running the war, Mary had taken charge of redecorating the White House. Congress had appropriated $20,000 to repair the White House and buy new furnishings, and Mary, who prior to this time had never been responsible for anything larger than a household budget, went on lavish shopping sprees in New York and Philadelphia. In a matter of months, she had spent the entire sum—which had been intended to last for four years. Lincoln, who rarely swore in anger, was furious when he found out, complaining that she had wasted so much money on "flub-dubs" for that "damned old house," which he said was already "better than any house they had ever lived in."

Congress eventually appropriated additional funds and hushed up the scandal, but Mary continued to pad expense accounts and clash with Lincoln's secretaries over money. Her constant quarreling and conniving with them over money earned her the nickname "the Hellcat" from

Nicolay and Hay. The secretaries had much more respect for Lincoln than for his wife, and their nickname for the president became "the Tycoon."

Mary loved to show off her sophisticated taste to the Washington elite at White House receptions. To keep up with fashion, she hired Elizabeth Keckley, a talented dressmaker and former slave who had sewn for other important residents of Washington. Lincoln, of course, knew nothing of fashion, but he liked to tease his wife about her extravagant ways. Once, prior to a White House reception, he commented on Mary's long-trained dress and low neckline, saying, "Whew! our cat has a long tail tonight! Mother, it is my opinion, if some of that tail was nearer the head, it would be in better style."

When he could get a break from official duties, Lincoln loved to tell little stories to his sons and the Taft boys. Julia Taft said that the boys would gather around him, and he'd tell them stories about pioneer life or fighting Indians. He also loved to roughhouse with the boys, and one day, Julia opened a door to find the president lying on his back on the floor with his sons and the two Taft brothers holding down his arms and legs. As soon as the boys saw her, Tad called out, "Julie, come quick and sit on his stomach!" Julia thought that to do *that* "would be like laying profane hands on the Lord's anointed," and just as any respectable student at Madame Smith's French School would, she *vanished.*

★ ★ ★

On the war front, General McClellan's luster had begun to fade. The weeks of training turned into months, and all McClellan wanted to do with the Army of the Potomac was to drill it and have parade reviews. Although he wasn't proving to be much of a fighter, McClellan was a good politician and managed to maneuver old General Scott out of his position as commander of the Union forces, getting himself appointed in his place. Becoming increasingly convinced that McClellan was reluctant to fight, the press and various political leaders in Washington began to clamor for a military campaign. The egotistic McClellan grew resentful of the politicians who criticized him and lost respect for virtually every politician— including Lincoln. He dismissed the president as "the original gorilla" and said he was "nothing more than a well-meaning baboon."

Lincoln probably knew of McClellan's insults but had supported the Young Napoleon, as the general was called, anyway. He had assured McClellan that he would have sufficient time for preparation and drill of the army. But by mid-November 1861, it was obvious that the general would not be launching an eastern military campaign against the Confederacy before winter set in.

Lincoln finally realized that he had placed too much confidence in McClellan and protected him too diligently from criticism, and in doing so, he had aided McClellan's growing sense of contempt for the government. This contempt turned to insult when Lincoln, Secretary of State Seward, and John Hay went to McClellan's home one night to talk to him. They arrived before the general returned and, after conversing with the servant, decided to wait for him in the parlor. When McClellan came home later, rather than greeting the president and his party, he simply walked past the parlor and went upstairs to bed.

As if things weren't bad enough for Lincoln, in December, McClellan contracted typhoid and confined himself to bed. In a meeting in early January 1862 with Quartermaster General Montgomery Meigs, Lincoln said despondently, "General, what shall I do? The people are impatient; Chase has no money and he tells me he can raise no more; the General of the Army has typhoid fever. The bottom is out of the tub. What shall I do?"

Lincoln soon came up with an answer to his own question.

SHOVELING FLEAS
1862

In January 1862, Lincoln finally lost patience with McClellan's sick leave and called a meeting of Little Mac's senior commanders to inquire as to what the general's plans were. He told them that if McClellan did not intend to use the army, "he would like to borrow it." McClellan got wind of this meeting and roused himself from his sick bed to come to a follow-up meeting with the president, where he refused to divulge to Lincoln his plans for the spring offensive unless the president ordered him to. Reluctant to do that, Lincoln nevertheless concluded that he would have to be more forceful with McClellan in the future. He decided to take steps to increase discipline in the War Department.

He started by firing the unscrupulous secretary of war, Simon Cameron. He replaced him with Edwin Stanton, a "War Democrat" who had been a very capable attorney general in the closing months of the Buchanan administration. Lincoln had met Stanton back in 1855, when he was co-counsel with him on a legal case in Ohio. Stanton had insulted Lincoln during that encounter, however, and called him a "long-armed ape" behind his back. Never one to hold grudges, Lincoln decided Stanton was the best man to run the army and put him in charge of the War Department in mid-January.

Stanton was, to put it mildly, an irascible individual. But he was intelligent, an efficient administrator, as ferocious as a bulldog, a workaholic, and—like Lincoln—scrupulously honest. He put an abrupt end to Cameron's questionable practices and brought a new sense of order and energy to the War Department.

While Lincoln was replacing Cameron, some leading Republican senators thought it was a good time to replace additional cabinet members. Lincoln disagreed but listened patiently to them, and when the senators had finished their argument, he said:

> Gentlemen, your request for a change of the whole Cabinet reminds me of a story I once heard in Illinois, of a farmer who was bothered by skunks. His wife insisted on his trying to get rid of them. He loaded his shotgun one moonlit night and awaited developments. After some time the wife heard the shotgun go off, and in a few minutes the farmer entered the house.
>
> "What luck have you?" asked she.
>
> "I hid myself behind the wood-pile," said the old man,

"with the shotgun pointed towards the hen roost, and 'fore long there appeared not one skunk, but seven. I took aim, blazed away, killed one, and he raised such a fearful smell I concluded it was best to let the other six go."

Lincoln did not replace any other cabinet members.

In addition to the political and military pressure, the abolitionists started to increase pressure on Lincoln to free the slaves. Lawyer and diarist George Templeton Strong went to Lincoln to encourage emancipation and later recounted Lincoln's response:

> Wa-al, that reminds me of a party of Methodist parsons that was traveling in Illinois when I was a boy thar, and they had a branch to cross that was pretty bad—ugly to cross, ye know, because the waters was up. And they got considerin' and discussin' how they should git across it, and they talked about it for two hours, and one of 'em thought they had ought to cross one way when they got there, and another another way, and they got quarrelin' about it, till at last an old brother put in, and he says, says he, "Brethren, this here talk ain't no use. I never cross a river until I come to it."

In other words, Lincoln was not yet ready for emancipation.

But at last General McClellan was ready—not to free the slaves, but to attack Richmond—and revealed his plan for the spring offensive to Lincoln. Rather than marching the army due south, as everyone expected, he proposed to use a large naval force to transport the army down the Chesapeake Bay, land it at Fort Monroe, and move up the Virginia Peninsula. Although Lincoln had his reservations, he had been educating himself on military science and saw advantages in McClellan's plan. He finally accepted it and decided to stay in constant contact with McClellan during the campaign.

Lincoln stayed in close contact with the war's progress via the telegraph. Two or three times a day, nearly every day of the war, he took short walks to the War Department Building to visit the telegraph operators' room. He enjoyed these outings, not only because he could get the latest news, but because he also liked to escape the pressures of the White House and relax with the young officers who sent the messages. Upon arriving, he would go to the drawer that had the latest telegrams and, proceeding from top to bottom, read them all. In his first few visits, he would say, after reading for a while, "Well boys, I am down to raisins," and quit. After they had heard this expression a number of times, one of them asked him what he meant.

In explanation, Lincoln told the story of "the little girl who celebrated her birthday by eating very freely of many good things, topping off with raisins for dessert. During the night, she was taken violently ill, and when the doctor arrived, she was busy casting up her accounts. The genial doctor, scrutinizing the contents of the vessel, noticed some small black objects that had just appeared and remarked to the anxious parent that all danger was past, because the child was 'down to raisins.' 'So,' Lincoln said, 'when I reach the message in this pile which I saw on my last visit, I know that I need go no further.'"

Lincoln also told the telegraph operators the story of a well-dressed man who, upon arriving in a theater, found an empty seat beside him and placed his high silk hat on it, open side up. Becoming interested in the play, he failed to notice the approach of a fat, near-sighted dowager until she had plumped down upon it and he heard a crunching noise. Holding the flattened hat in front of him, he said, sadly, "Madam, I could have told you that my hat wouldn't fit before you tried it on."

Meanwhile, things had improved in the western theater. Even though Lincoln had not been successful in motivating the Department of the Ohio's General Buell to move southward in eastern Kentucky, he was pleased with the performance of the Department of the Missouri. The Department of the Missouri was commanded by General Henry "Old Brains" Halleck, who was the author of one of the books on military science Lincoln checked out from the Library of Congress. Although Halleck was an exceedingly cautious sort, he had a very bold subordinate commander, Brigadier General U. S. Grant. Grant—whose real name was Hiram Ulysses Grant—was a small, unassuming man and West Point graduate who had fought bravely in the Mexican-American War. At the beginning of the Civil War, he was appointed colonel of an Illinois regiment and soon developed the reputation of a being a skilled, determined fighter.

The Confederates had built two forts in northwestern Kentucky, Fort Henry along the Tennessee River and Fort Donelson along the parallel Cumberland River, to guard against invasion by the Yankees along those water routes. Grant assembled an attacking force of fifteen thousand men and seven ironclad gunboats, and on February 1, 1862, he moved south. He took Fort Henry on February 6 and Fort Donelson ten days later, capturing more than twelve thousand Confederate prisoners. Prior to surrendering, the Confederate commander had asked for terms, which Grant refused. He said the surrender must be unconditional, and the newspapers started calling him "Unconditional Surrender" Grant. He quickly became a national hero.

With their two primary strongpoints gone, the Confederate forces in western Kentucky retreated all the way to northern Mississippi. With relatively few casualties, Grant had swallowed a Confederate army whole and secured Kentucky for the Union. He loaded his army onto transports and moved farther south via the Tennessee River. They encamped in southwestern Tennessee at Pittsburg Landing, near Shiloh Church, and waited for reinforcements to arrive from General Buell's army. The Confederates retreated all the way to Corinth, Mississippi, where they rested and regrouped their forces.

Although Grant's victories in February were good news for Lincoln, he and Mary were alarmed when both Willie and Tad contracted typhoid fever. Both boys were confined to bed, and Willie, whose condition was worse, steadily declined. Willie called for his friend Bud Taft, who came to his bedside and stayed there most of the time he was sick. Lincoln and Mary also spent a great deal of time with both boys, and on February 20, Willie seemed to get better for a while. But then, at 5:00 p.m. that day, Willie died. Lincoln entered John Nicolay's office and, sobbing aloud, told his secretary, "My boy is gone—he is actually gone!"

Mary became hysterical. She secluded herself for weeks in her bedroom, weeping and refusing to comfort Tad, who was still quite sick. Lincoln dealt with the funeral and the nursing of his youngest son with little help from his wife. Unfortunately for Tad, Mary could not stand to have the Taft boys around anymore because they reminded her of Willie. So in the future, Tad's father would make an earnest effort to become his youngest son's best friend.

While Mary was incapacitated, Rebecca Pomroy, a nurse Lincoln said was "one of the best women he ever knew," stayed in the White House to help take care of Tad. She comforted Mary and the president as much as she could, talked to him about her faith, and expressed her dream to hold a prayer meeting in the hospital where she nursed soldiers. Lincoln appreciated her company and talked freely about the Bible with her. He told her that the Psalms "were the best," for he found in them "something for every day in the week." He also acknowledged his need for "the prayers of many" and concurred that a prayer meeting for the patients at the hospital would be a good idea, because the country needed "more praying and less swearing."

Unlike Mary, Lincoln could not take time to grieve over the loss of Willie. On March 8, Lincoln and his cabinet received news that the recently constructed Confederate ironclad ship, the CSS *Virginia*, had attacked the North's blockading squadron at Hampton Roads, Virginia, sinking two ships and causing a third to run aground. The Northern ships were conventional wooden ones, but the *Virginia* was an ironclad, a new concept in naval engineering. The *Virginia* had been built from the remains of the North's USS *Merrimack*, which had been partially destroyed by fire.

Fortunately, the North had built an ironclad ship as well, and it arrived the night of March 8 to do battle with the *Virginia* the next day. The USS *Monitor* had been built in a mere 101 days, and its construction hadn't started until rumors began circulating that the Confederate navy was working on an ironclad ship at the Gosport Navy Yard southeast of Richmond. Although many had been skeptical of the *Monitor*'s merits, including Secretary of War Stanton, Lincoln supported its construction. When the *Monitor*'s developer, the celebrated engineer John Ericsson, had finished presenting the plans for his warship to Lincoln, the president quipped, "I feel like the girl who said when she put on her stocking 'There's something in that worth looking at!'"

At the cabinet meeting late in the afternoon of March 8, Secretary of the Navy Gideon Welles announced the *Monitor* would soon arrive and would fight the *Virginia* in the morning. But Secretary of War Stanton scoffed and belligerently declared that a small ship like the *Monitor*, with only two guns, would be unable to stop the twelve-gun *Virginia*.

The next day, on March 9, the two ironclads fought for about three hours. Although the *Virginia* outgunned the smaller *Monitor*, the latter was much more maneuverable, and the fight ended with neither ship being able to inflict significant damage on the other. Neither won a resounding victory, but the *Monitor* succeeded in preventing the *Virginia* from breaking the Union blockade. After the battle, the *Virginia* returned to her home at the Gosport Navy Yard for repairs, and the *Monitor* returned to her blockade station at Hampton Roads. The *Virginia* was later scuttled to prevent its capture by General McClellan's forces, so the ironclads never met in battle again.

Stanton's vociferous criticism of the *Monitor* at the March 8 cabinet meeting had proven unjustified. Lincoln was frequently amused by his excitable secretary of war, and when he appointed him to his office, he had compared him to a preacher who "was in the habit of going off on such high flights at camp meetings that they had to put bricks in his pockets to keep him down. He added, 'I may have to do that with Stanton, but if I do, bricks in his pocket will be better than bricks in his hat. I'll risk him for a while without either.'"

Although Lincoln usually let Stanton run the War Department the way he wanted, he would occasionally override him on an issue such as a political appointment or a soldier's court-martial for desertion. Once, a delegation that Lincoln had sent to Stanton with orders to grant their request returned with a complaint. Not only had Stanton refused to grant their request, but he had actually called Lincoln a fool for sending such an order. Lincoln, feigning astonishment, inquired, "Did Stanton call me a fool?" When this was confirmed, he remarked, "Well, I guess I had better go over and see Stanton about *this*. Stanton is usually right."

★ ★ ★

The year 1862 would become the transition year for the North's purpose of waging war. At the war's inception, Lincoln knew that the Northern people's primary motivation was to preserve the Union rather than to fight against slavery. Lincoln concurred that preservation of the Union was paramount, but he also continued to hope that the people would one day "return to the principles of the Declaration of Independence," and support the elimination of slavery.

Lincoln realized that the South's slaves were a significant resource, and the labor they provided behind the lines allowed the Confederacy to put a higher percentage of men into the army. If that source of manpower could be removed, it would weaken the South's ability to wage war. But his dilemma in regard to emancipation was twofold. First, to completely eliminate slavery would require an amendment to the Constitution, something that was politically impossible in 1862. Second, the Northern people did not appreciate how much its elimination would help in the war effort, and in early 1862, only a minority of Northerners thought that the elimination of slavery was a cause worth risking their lives for.

After consulting with Attorney General Edward Bates, Lincoln determined that as president during time of rebellion, he could legally confiscate any of the South's resources that were enabling its resistance. Consequently, he could weaken the Confederacy by refusing to return the slaves who escaped their masters when Northern armies advanced through Southern territory. It was Lincoln's hope that as the Northern people saw this benefit of emancipation, support for an amendment to the Constitution would grow.

A secondary benefit of emancipation would be the effect of lessening any chance that Great Britain would intervene in the war on behalf of the Confederacy. The South's diplomats in London were working diligently toward that goal, pointing out that no matter which side won the war, slavery would remain intact. If the elimination of slavery was added to the North's war goals, Great Britain could no longer morally justify their intervention on behalf of the proslavery South.

But the spring of 1862 was still too early for the issuance of an emancipation proclamation. Lincoln had to wait until the border states—all of which had slaves—were more formally committed to the Union. He watched the political situation carefully, waiting for his opportunity.

About this time, a group of ministers from Chicago met with Lincoln in the White House to encourage him to free the slaves. Lincoln told them that the nation wasn't ready for that step yet and politely asked them to leave. As the ministers were filing out, one of them felt it his duty to make a final appeal to the president's conscience. He turned and said to Lincoln, "What you have said to us, Mr. President, compels me to say to you in reply that it is a message to you from our Divine Master, through me, commanding you, sir, to open the doors of bondage that the slave may go free."

Lincoln patiently replied, "That may be sir, for I have studied this question, by night and by day, for weeks and for months. But if it is, as you say, a message from the Divine Master, is it not odd that the only channel He could send it by was from the roundabout route of that awful, wicked city of Chicago?"

In late March, McClellan finally began his long awaited Peninsula Campaign. Transferring his army via transport, he landed it at Fort Monroe, on the peninsula between the York and James Rivers, about eighty miles southeast of Richmond. From there, he began a gradual movement up the peninsula toward the Confederate capital, slowly pushing back the Confederate army. Deluded into believing he was outnumbered, McClellan advanced too cautiously and lost the initiative. Confederate

General Johnston saw an opportunity to attack at an advantage and forced McClellan to retreat back down the peninsula.

General Johnston was wounded in battle, and Jefferson Davis replaced him with General Robert E. Lee. Lee continued the attacks and, by July, had finally pushed McClellan and the Army of the Potomac back to a defensive position at Harrison's Landing along the James River.

In the coming weeks, McClellan sent a continuous barrage of telegrams to Stanton, demanding more reinforcements so that he might advance on Richmond again. McClellan's constant complaining that he didn't have enough troops caused Lincoln to wisecrack that sending men to the general "is like shoveling fleas across a barnyard—half of them never get there."

In the early stages of the Peninsula Campaign, Stanton and Lincoln traveled to Fort Monroe to inspect McClellan's army. Stanton told Lincoln how, just before their departure from Washington, he had received an unclear telegram from a general who demanded his immediate response to a plan. Stanton didn't have time to research it and simply responded, "All right, go ahead." Lincoln replied:

> I suppose you meant that it was all right if it was good for him, and all wrong if it was not. That reminds me of a story about a horse that was sold at the cross-roads near where I once lived. The horse was supposed to be fast, and quite a number of people were present at the time appointed for the

sale. A small boy was employed to ride the horse backward and forward to exhibit his points. One of the would-be buyers followed the boy down the road and asked him confidentially if the horse had a splint. "Well, mister," said the boy, "if it's good for him he has got it, but if it isn't good for him, he hasn't."

Things continued to go well for the North in the western theater of the war. General Grant had been promoted from brigadier to major general, and General Halleck had been promoted to command of all Union forces in Tennessee, including those of the recalcitrant General Buell. But on April 6, 1862, Confederate forces under command of General Albert Sidney Johnston attacked Grant's army along the Tennessee River at Shiloh Church. Grant's army was totally surprised by the attack and was pushed back nearly to the banks of the Tennessee River. But Grant received reinforcements from Buell overnight and counterattacked on April 7. The Confederates lost the second day's battle and retreated back to Corinth, Mississippi.

The desperate, two-day Battle of Shiloh resulted in a staggering twenty-five thousand casualties between the two sides. Grant's critics claimed that he had been negligent—or even drunk—and demanded his resignation. But Lincoln, pleased with Grant's aggressiveness, doggedly supported his general.

Soon after the Battle of Shiloh, Secretary of the Navy Welles met with

Lincoln to suggest the idea of capturing the important Confederate port of New Orleans at the mouth of the Mississippi River. New Orleans was the Confederacy's second largest city and most important port for trade with Europe, so Lincoln ordered Welles to develop a well-thought-out plan. He illustrated his desire with a story:

> There was an old woman in Illinois who missed some of her chickens and couldn't imagine what had become of them. Someone suggested that they had been carried off by a skunk; so she told her husband he must sit up that night and shoot the critter. The old man sat up all night and next morning came in with two pet rabbits. "Thar," he said, "your chickens are all safe; thar's two of them skunks I killed."
>
> "Them ain't skunks," said the old woman, "them's my pet rabbits; you allers was a fool!"
>
> "Well, then," returned the old man, "if them ain't skunks I don't know a skunk when I sees it."
>
> Now, Mr. Secretary, the navy has been hunting pet rabbits long enough; suppose you send 'em after skunks.

Per Lincoln's orders, a combined Union army/navy operation captured New Orleans at the end of April. After this victory, the next step would be to capture the Confederate stronghold of Vicksburg, about two hundred miles north of New Orleans on the banks of the Mississippi River. Lincoln was anxious to open up the Mississippi River for commerce.

With an eye toward trade with Europe, Seward and Lincoln continued their efforts to patch up relations with the British and forget the conflict over the *Trent* affair. While entertaining British magazine correspondent Edward Dicey, Seward lit up a cigar and told their guest that he regretted to say the president had few vices, in that he neither drank nor smoked. Lincoln quickly rejoined, "That is a doubtful compliment. I recollect once being outside a stage in Illinois, and a man sitting by me offered me a cigar. I told him I had no vices. He said nothing, smoked for some time, and then grunted out, 'It's my experience in life that folks who have got no vices have plaguy few virtues.'"

McClellan continued to demand more troops, so Lincoln went to Harrison's Landing to assess the condition of the army for himself. After talking to McClellan, officers, and men, he concluded that although the army was in good shape, McClellan was doubtful about attacking Richmond again—regardless of how many reinforcements he received.

While Lincoln was visiting, McClellan read to the president a dispatch from a subordinate commander who had obviously exaggerated the fierceness of a recent battle. This triggered from Lincoln a story about a notorious liar: "[The man had] attained such a reputation as an exaggerator that he finally instructed his servant to stop him, when his tongue was running too rapidly, by pulling his coat or touching his feet.

{ *Harper's Weekly*, September 17, 1864 }

This September 17, 1864, cartoon from *Harper's Weekly* reminded readers of General McClellan's 1862 Peninsula Campaign against Richmond, where the general's over-cautious tendency to repeatedly entrench his army caused him to lose the initiative to the Confederate defenders.

One day, the master was relating the wonders he had seen in Europe and described a building which was about a mile long and a half-mile high." Suddenly, when the servant's heel came crashing down on the narrator's toes, he stopped abruptly. When one of the listeners asked how broad this incredible building might be, the red-faced narrator modestly replied, "About a foot!"

McClellan's bewilderment as to what to do about Richmond prompted Lincoln to start relating a similar story of a man in Illinois "who, in company with a number of friends, visited the state penitentiary. They wandered all through the institution and saw everything, but when it was time to depart, the man became separated from his friends and couldn't find his way out. He roamed up and down one corridor after another, becoming more desperate all the time, when, at last, he came across a convict who was looking out from between the bars of his cell door. Here was salvation at last! Hurrying up to the prisoner, he hastily asked, 'Say! How do you get out of this place?'"

To discuss the military situation, Lincoln went to see Secretary Stanton. When the president arrived, Stanton set aside some documents he was about to review, saying they weren't very important and could wait. This brought to the president's mind a story about a Colonel Fisk in Missouri. When the colonel had taken over command, "he informed the men that he would do all the swearing for the regiment. They agreed, as they had to, and for some time, no one heard any profanity around camp. Then one day, John Todd, a teamster, encountered several miles of mudholes, each one worse than the one before. About midway along this road, Todd let go a flood of cussing that reached Fisk's ears. The Colonel called John into his tent and said, 'Look here, John, didn't you agree to let me do all the cussing for this regiment?'

"'Yes, Colonel, I did,' John answered, 'but this job of cussing had to be done right there and then, and I couldn't see you anywhere around to do it.'"

Lincoln told Stanton that the point of the story was that "anything which comes up today must be done today in order to finish this war."

The taciturn Stanton considered Lincoln's storytelling to be below the dignity of the office of the chief executive and rarely laughed at Lincoln's jokes. The president would occasionally start cabinet meetings by reading aloud something funny from one of his favorite humorists, such as Artemus Ward or Petroleum V. Nasby. Once, when Lincoln was the only one who laughed at what he had read, he chided his cabinet, saying, "Gentlemen, why don't you laugh? With the fearful strain that is upon me night and day, if I did not laugh I should die, and you need this medicine as much as I do."

Now that he was certain McClellan had lost his nerve, Lincoln decided to bring two generals from the western theater to take charge in the East. Grant's commanding officer, Henry W. Halleck, was brought to Washington to act as the new commanding general of all Union armies. One of Grant's peers, General John Pope, was brought east to take over the Union's newly formed Army of Virginia near Washington. Pope, not much of a diplomat, managed to offend not only the Southern people, but a lot of the Northern soldiers as well with his pronouncement that he was coming to them from the West, where he had usually seen the enemy in retreat, and that his headquarters would "be in the saddle." Of course this caused more than one wag to observe that this meant Pope's "headquarters [was going to be] where his hindquarters should be."

Pope made plans to march from Washington toward Richmond and was assured that McClellan would send him reinforcements from the Army of the Potomac. On August 3, 1862, Halleck ordered McClellan to start shipping troops northward to join Pope, but McClellan did not begin his redeployment until August 14.

In early June 1862, Lincoln concluded that the border states had become sufficiently committed to the Union to allow him to announce his intention to emancipate the slaves. He wanted to do this soon, because his ambassador to Great Britain, Charles Francis Adams, warned him that the British government was getting closer to intervening in the war, an action that would benefit the South.

Lincoln decided to start drafting his emancipation document. In order to avoid the various distractions of the White House, he worked on the draft in the telegraph operator's room at the War Department. He kept the document locked in a drawer there and worked on it for several weeks.

On July 13, Lincoln informed Secretary Seward and Secretary Welles of his decision to free the slaves, and a week later, he took his draft document from its hiding place in the telegraph office and presented it to his entire cabinet for their review.

The Emancipation Proclamation would act as a war measure, freeing slaves currently within Confederate lines in order to weaken the rebellion. Most of the cabinet, including Secretary Seward, supported it. But Seward suggested that since the war had been going badly in the East, they should wait until the North had won a significant battle, so it wouldn't appear that it was "our last shriek, on retreat." Lincoln agreed and put it away, waiting for a military success.

In mid-August, *New-York Tribune* editor Horace Greeley wrote an editorial calling for Lincoln to free the slaves. Lincoln responded with a carefully worded letter, which was published in the *Tribune* on August 22. Although he had already decided to free the slaves, he wanted to speak to those Northerners who were not yet convinced that it was the right thing to do. With this reply, he announced that he would only free the slaves if he reached the conclusion it was an act essential to the preservation of the Union:

I would save the Union. I would save it the shortest way under the Constitution. The sooner the national authority can be restored; the nearer the Union will be "the Union as it was." If there be those who would not save the Union, unless they could at the same time save slavery, I do not agree with them. If there be those who would not save the Union unless they could at the same time destroy slavery, I do not agree with them. My paramount object in this struggle is to save the Union, and is not either to save or to destroy slavery. If I could save the Union without freeing any slave I would do it, and if I could save it by freeing all the slaves I would do it; and if I could save it by freeing some and leaving others alone I would also do that. What I do about slavery, and the colored race, I do because I believe it helps to save the Union; and what I forbear, I forbear because I do not believe it would help to save the Union. I shall do less whenever I shall believe what I am doing hurts the cause, and I shall do more whenever I shall believe doing more will help the cause. I shall try to correct errors when shown to be errors; and I shall adopt new views so fast as they shall appear to be true views.

I have here stated my purpose according to my view of official duty; and I intend no modification of my oft-expressed personal wish that all men everywhere could be free.

While Lincoln contemplated emancipation, Confederate general Robert E. Lee went on the offensive, having concluded that McClellan was not going to pose any further threat to Richmond from the Peninsula. He left a small force entrenched between McClellan and Richmond and marched most of his army northward to attack General Pope south of Washington. The Army of Northern Virginia, as Lee called it, met up with Pope's Army of Virginia at the old Manassas battlefield on August 28 and 29. Attacked first by General Stonewall Jackson's force and then by General James Longstreet's, Pope never even knew what hit him. McClellan had reluctantly sent Pope a few reinforcements, thinking selfishly that Pope should "get out of his own scrape," but the troops were too few, and too late. Pope was soundly defeated at Second Manassas and soon found himself on a train, westward bound, to fight Indians.

Having suffered another inglorious defeat, the Union troops around Washington became quite dejected. Lincoln knew that only one general could reinstill confidence into the army. Reluctantly, on September 1, against the wishes of both Stanton and the radicals of Congress, Lincoln combined the remnants of Pope's army with the Army of the Potomac and put McClellan in command of both near Washington.

To take advantage of his victory over Pope, Confederate President Davis decided to attack northward in both the East and West, sending General Lee into Maryland and General Braxton Bragg into eastern Kentucky. Anxious about the future, Lincoln said in a cabinet meeting about this time that he had made a covenant with God that if the Union army won a victory, he would issue the Emancipation Proclamation.

Lincoln had good reason for praying, because General Lee and his army were in their prime. Lee had brilliant infantry commanders with Jackson and Longstreet and an unmatched cavalry commander in Jeb Stuart. Lee skillfully moved his army northward, keeping its position masked by South Mountain and Stuart's cavalry. The Confederate commander knew his adversary well and had no reason to expect McClellan to act aggressively.

But Lee had not reckoned on Lincoln's prayer, which evidently was answered when a couple of McClellan's men accidentally found a lost copy of Lee's invasion plans in a field vacated by Confederate cavalry. These plans gave McClellan the complete details of Lee's invasion route and disposition of his forces. Through them, McClellan discovered that Lee's army was spread over a vast distance. He realized if he acted quickly, he could break through one of South Mountain's passes and attack the Confederate army before Lee could concentrate all of his forces.

But Lee smelled a rat and quickly assembled his forces at Sharpsburg, Maryland. On September 17, the two armies met there and fought a horrific battle, known as the Battle of Antietam, which resulted in more than twenty-five thousand casualties between the two sides. Lee's invasion was halted, and within two days, he began his retreat to Virginia.

Lee successfully pulled his army back across the Potomac River, and Lincoln, though disappointed over Lee's escape, accepted this as the victory he had been asking for. He issued the preliminary Emancipation Proclamation on September 22. The proclamation stated that if, by the first of the year, the Southern states had not returned to the Union, he would issue a final proclamation that would free all the slaves in the areas still in rebellion at that time.

The terrible suffering and casualties caused Lincoln to increasingly ponder God's purpose in the war. He recorded his thoughts about this subject soon after issuing the preliminary Emancipation Proclamation. In a private note, prescient of his second inaugural address, he wrote:

> The will of God prevails. In great contests each party claims to act in accordance with the will of God. Both may be, and one must be, wrong. God cannot be for and against the same thing at the same time. In the present civil war it is quite possible that God's purpose is something different from the purpose of either party; and yet the human instrumentalities, working just as they do, are of the best adaptation to effect his purpose. I am almost ready to say that this is probably true; that God wills this contest, and wills that it shall not end yet.

After the Battle of Antietam, McClellan kept the Army of the Potomac in Maryland, refusing to pursue Lee into Virginia, and Lincoln became increasingly impatient with him. On October 24, Lincoln responded to a request from McClellan for additional horses. Lincoln telegraphed, "I have just read your dispatch about sore tongued and fatigued horses. Will you pardon me for asking what the horses of your army have done since the battle of Antietam that fatigue anything?"

Another example of Lincoln's increasing contempt for McClellan was when he went to visit the Army of the Potomac in camp. Gazing at the army encampment in the distance, Lincoln rhetorically asked his friend Ozias Hatch what it was he saw before them. Hatch responded that it was the Army of the Potomac. Lincoln said, "No, you are mistaken; that is General McClellan's bodyguard."

Northern reaction to the preliminary Emancipation Proclamation was mixed. While those who hated slavery rejoiced, many Democrats denounced it as an act that would promote a dangerous slave uprising. The press's reaction ran the gambit too, with Democratic organs being the most outspoken against it. Although some soldiers were angered and talked about marching on Washington, McClellan told his army the best way to correct things would be "at the polls" in November.

One of the most important reactions to the Emancipation Proclamation was from the government of Great Britain. Prior to the issuance of the preliminary proclamation, the British government was on the verge of recognizing the Confederacy and offering to mediate a truce. But after the North won the battle of Antietam and Lincoln issued the proclamation, the British cabinet decided to hold off on any intervention and wait for further developments. They never seriously considered intervention again.[1]

Peace Democrats, who opposed the war, wanted an immediate peace settlement with the Confederacy. They were nicknamed by the Republicans "Copperheads" after the venomous snake, and were the most vocal in their denunciation of Lincoln and the Emancipation Proclamation. The Democratic Party made gains in the fall elections, picking up more than thirty seats in the House of Representatives. Although this was bad news for Republicans, it was not a clear defeat, since the Republican Party still controlled both houses of Congress. But in the midst of this bad political news, Lincoln at least had one satisfaction. He appointed his old friend, Yale-educated Judge David Davis, to the U.S. Supreme Court.

On November 5, the day after the elections, Lincoln fired McClellan and replaced him with General Ambrose Burnside, one of McClellan's corps commanders. Burnside certainly looked the soldier. He had distinctive facial hair that completely covered his portly cheeks, and his style of beard would eventually spawn the term "sideburns." Burnside was an honorable subordinate officer, but his ability to command an entire army was still unknown.

Lincoln also took action to improve things in the western theater of the war. He did this by removing General Buell who, like McClellan, had been reluctant to wage the sort of aggressive war that the president

---

1. For British contemplation of intervention, see Jones, *Union in Peril*, chapters 8–10.

believed was necessary to defeat the South. He replaced Buell with General William Rosecrans, who was an avid supporter of Lincoln's hard-hitting war policies.

Meanwhile, General Grant had begun the task of capturing the last significant Confederate stronghold on the Mississippi River at Vicksburg, Mississippi. Initially, Grant had tried marching overland from Corinth, Mississippi, but his supply lines had proven too vulnerable to General Nathan Bedford Forrest's Confederate cavalry. So Grant decided he would focus in the coming months on taking Vicksburg by way of the water route—the Mississippi River.

In the East, things got worse for the Army of the Potomac after McClellan left. On December 13, McClellan's replacement General Burnside proved himself totally incompetent as an army commander at the Battle of Fredericksburg, Virginia. Burnside sent his troops repeatedly against the strongest point of the Confederate line, where Longstreet's First Corps was safely protected in a sunken road behind a stone wall. Longstreet, who had many friends in the Union army, including General Grant out west, would later say, "A series of braver, more desperate charges than those hurled against the troops in the sunken road was never known, and the piles and cross-piles of [Union] dead marked a field such as I never saw before or since." The Army of the Potomac suffered more than thirteen thousand casualties at Fredericksburg, nearly triple the number of Confederate casualties.

After the battle, the army's morale plummeted and desertions rose significantly. Lincoln was in agony over the casualties, saying, "If there is a worse place than hell, I am in it." The army, the press, and the Democratic Party denounced this failure of military leadership.

At the same time as this military catastrophe, Lincoln was facing a political crisis as well. Treasury Secretary Chase, who continued to yearn for Lincoln's job, found in recent events an opportunity to criticize Lincoln's management of the war. He told members of Congress that the president spent too much time listening to Secretary of State Seward and not enough time conferring with the rest of the cabinet. He claimed that cabinet meetings were a waste of time, and Lincoln did not ask his cabinet's input on significant issues. Lincoln realized that this was simply a power grab by Chase, who wanted to get rid of his main cabinet rival, the secretary of state. Seward offered his resignation, hoping this might help Lincoln, but the president demurred. When congressional leaders asked to meet with Lincoln in the White House, he envisioned a way to get through this challenge.

Lincoln did not want congressional leadership interfering with his cabinet, and he knew that to lose Seward would be to sacrifice power to them. Consequently, he invited the entire cabinet, minus Seward, to be present when the congressional leaders came to talk to him. When the congressmen presented Chase's objections, Lincoln denied their significance. He said that issues were discussed openly in his cabinet and asked if anyone in the cabinet disagreed. No one, including the embarrassed Chase, said anything to the contrary. Disgusted with Chase's duplicity, the congressional leaders dropped the issue and departed.

The next day, the humiliated Chase reluctantly offered his resignation too. Gleefully, Lincoln snatched it from his hand and said, "Now I can ride, I've got a pumpkin in each end of my bag!" Since he had resignation letters from both Seward and Chase, he could decline them both and get the congressional leadership off his back. Chase had been politically outmaneuvered and dolefully returned to his position in the Treasury Department.

Although Lincoln loved swapping stories with men, he was still uncomfortable talking to women. But occasionally he would joke with one, such as when the beautiful stage actress Rose Eytinge visited the White House. Lincoln said to her, "So this is the little lady that all us folks in Washington like so much. Don't you ever come 'round here asking me to do some of those impossible things you women always ask for, for I would have to do it, and then I'd get into trouble."

Even though progress on the war front in the eastern theater had been poor, Lincoln was able to look back on the year of 1862 as being one of momentous achievement in the nonmilitary realm. He had not only issued the preliminary Emancipation Proclamation, but he had also signed into law several significant bills enacted by Congress. These included the Pacific Railway Act, which started the construction of the transcontinental railroad, the Homestead Act, which gave 160 acres of farmland to anyone willing to work it, the Legal Tender Act, which authorized the use of paper notes to pay the government's huge bills resulting from the Civil War, and the Morrill Act, which allowed for the creation of land-grant colleges—which today are represented by many of the state universities across the nation.

On December 1, 1862, Lincoln delivered a synopsis of the year's events in his annual message to Congress. He closed the speech with the following exhortation to the nation's leaders:

> Fellow-citizens, we cannot escape history. We of this Congress and this administration will be remembered in spite of ourselves. No personal significance, or insignificance, can spare one or another of us. The fiery trial through which we pass, will light us down, in honor or dishonor, to the latest generation…We—even we here—hold the power, and bear the responsibility. In giving freedom to the slave, we assure freedom to the free—honorable alike in what we give, and what we preserve. We shall nobly save, or meanly lose, the last best, hope of earth. Other means may succeed; this could not fail. The way is plain, peaceful, generous, just—a way which, if followed, the world will forever applaud, and God must forever bless.

THE TYCOON
1863

New Year's Day, 1863—the long-awaited day for Lincoln to sign the final Emancipation Proclamation—finally arrived. The reception line of politicians, dignitaries, and well-wishers at the White House was a long one, and Lincoln had shaken so many hands that when it came time to sign the proclamation, his hand was swollen and weak, and he was afraid it would tremble. When he took up the pen with which he was to sign the document, he said, "I never, in my life, felt more certain that I was doing right, than I do in signing this paper." He usually signed documents with a simple "A. Lincoln," but for the Emancipation Proclamation, he proudly penned his full name.

The Emancipation Proclamation proclaimed that slaves in rebellion states would now be "thenceforward, and forever free." Critics said that it really freed no one, since the only slaves declared technically free were the ones currently outside of the control of the federal government. But this was a specious argument, and somewhere between twenty and fifty thousand slaves in the Union-occupied regions of Tennessee and along the Carolina coasts were freed immediately. Black people everywhere rejoiced, because they knew that as Union armies advanced further, millions of additional slaves would be emancipated.

Abolitionist and former slave Frederick Douglass was aware of the technical limitations of the document, but he and other antislavery activists also realized its significance. He said that its spirit had "a life and power far beyond its letter." Douglass had been encouraging Lincoln, through speeches and writings, to enlist black men in the army. The president began doing this in earnest after the first of January, and by the end of the war almost 180,000 black men would be recruited into the army and navy—nearly seven percent of the total enlistments.

In early March 1863, Lincoln heard that Confederate guerrilla leader John S. Mosby and his men had captured a Union general named E. H. Stoughton, along with a number of horses, at Fairfax Courthouse, Virginia. Stoughton had snoozed a little too late one Sunday morning, and Mosby walked into his bedroom and gave him a slap on the rear. Upon being so rudely awakened, the Union general shouted, "Do you know who I am?"

Mosby snickered, "Do you know Mosby, General?"

"Yes! Have you got the rascal?"

"No, but he has got *you!*"

The Confederates quickly rode away with their captives. When told of the incident, Lincoln couldn't resist saying that he did not mind the loss of the brigadier general as much as he did the loss of the horses. "I can make a much better brigadier general in five minutes," he said. "But those horses cost a hundred and twenty-five dollars apiece."

Debacles like the Battle of Fredericksburg and roaming of Confederate guerrillas behind the Union lines helped Lincoln realize that the Union commander in Virginia, General Burnside, would have to go. Lincoln decided to replace him with one of the corps commanders of the Army of the Potomac, General Joseph Hooker. Although he was considered a hard fighter, he was also a boastful, indiscreet officer who had loudly proclaimed that to win the war, the country needed a dictator.

On January 26, Lincoln summoned Hooker to Washington, gave him command, and handed the general a letter full of sage advice. Lincoln wrote, among other things, "I have heard, in such way as to believe it, of your recently saying that both the Army and the Government needed a Dictator. Of course it was not for this, but in spite of it, that I have given you the command. Only those generals who gain successes can set up dictators. What I now ask of you is military success, and I will risk the dictatorship."

Like McClellan, Hooker was a good organizer and he knew how to restore morale to the Army of the Potomac. He organized the commissary so that better food was provided, gave each corps its own unique insignia in order to instill some esprit de corps, and simplified the army's command structure. His actions instilled new pride in the Army of the Potomac, and desertions dropped significantly. He called the Army of the Potomac "the finest army on the planet" and bragged of how he would defeat Lee.

Lincoln was concerned about Hooker's braggadocio and set up a direct line of communication between Hooker and himself. Lincoln's own military skills had increased significantly during the war, and he frequently had a better grasp of the strategic situation than his military commanders did. When Hooker talked about capturing Richmond, Lincoln pointed out to his general that his primary objective should be Lee's army, *not* the Confederate capital.

Having twice as many men as Lee had, on April 27, Hooker took most of his army on a westward march to outflank the Confederates. But Lee discerned Hooker's plan and split his own army not once but twice in order to outflank him. The resulting fight, known as the Battle of Chancellorsville, was a brilliant victory for the South. But the victory came at a high price— Confederate General Jackson was wounded at Chancellorsville and would soon die of pneumonia while recovering.

Lincoln was devastated by the news of the thirty thousand casualties and Hooker's failure. He did what he could to support his general, but when Lee subsequently decided to invade the North again and Hooker did not aggressively oppose him, Lincoln demoted him back to corps command. Lincoln immediately appointed General George Gordon Meade, who was known as the "damned old goggle-eyed snapping turtle," to command of the Army of the Potomac.

While Hooker was failing Lincoln in the East, one of the western military commanders was causing problems too. After he had performed so miserably at the Battle of Fredericksburg, General Burnside had been sent west to take over command of the Department of the Ohio. Although this post was considered more "out of the way," he still managed to cause headaches for Lincoln. A few days after Hooker fought the Battle of Chancellorsville, Burnside arrested Copperhead congressman Clement Vallandigham at his home in Dayton, Ohio, because he had made a speech that the general considered subversive to the war effort. This arrest caused a tremendous outcry from the Democratic press, so in an effort to placate critics, Lincoln commuted Vallandigham's sentence from imprisonment to banishment to the Confederacy.

The Copperheads were not appeased and demanded that Vallandigham be allowed to return to Northern soil. But Lincoln refused and, in defending his action, pointed out that the congressman's rhetoric was inducing soldiers to desert the army—an offense punishable by firing squad. Lincoln insightfully asked, "Must I shoot a simple-minded soldier boy who deserts, while I must not touch a hair of a wily agitator who induces him to desert?"

While this quarrel was going on between the Copperheads and the president, Lee invaded Pennsylvania with an army of seventy thousand men. But the Union's old "snapping turtle" Meade lived up to his nickname and quickly rushed the Army of the Potomac northward to protect Washington. The two armies finally met up in south-central Pennsylvania, at a small town named Gettysburg.

For three days, from July 1 to July 3, the armies hammered each other at Gettysburg in what turned out to be, with more than fifty thousand casualties, the most costly battle of the war. Meade remained on the defensive, and Lee tried unsuccessfully to attack both of his opponent's flanks over the course of the first two days. On the final day, he hit the Union center with "Pickett's Charge," an attack that was unsuccessful. On July 5, having suffered more than twenty-five thousand casualties, Lee retreated to Virginia.

While Hooker and Meade were fighting Lee in Virginia and Pennsylvania, Grant had doggedly continued his campaign against the Confederate stronghold of Vicksburg. His first attack on the swampy northern side of the city had failed. He had tried other plans, including an effort to divert the Mississippi River away from Vicksburg by digging a canal, but they had not succeeded. Finally, in March 1863, Grant settled on a plan that would work.

Grant hit upon the idea of marching his army on the dry land of the western bank of the Mississippi to a point south of Vicksburg. Then, on a moonless night in mid-April, Admiral David Porter ran his gunboats and transports past the gauntlet of the Vicksburg batteries that guarded the Mississippi. Although the Confederate soldiers detected the boats and opened a tremendous fire, little damage was done to them, and they met Grant's army south of the city. The transports ferried Grant's troops from the western bank to the east, and Grant quickly marched his army northeast to attack the state capital of Jackson, Mississippi. After taking Jackson, he attacked westward toward Vicksburg. He soon had the Confederate troops bottled up in the trenches around Vicksburg. Grant decided to starve them out with a siege, and on July 4, the day after the Battle of Gettysburg ended in the east, the entire Confederate army of thirty thousand men in Vicksburg surrendered.

Lincoln recognized the significance of this victory, and when Union troops captured the last remaining Confederate outpost on the Mississippi a few days later, he wrote that "the Father of Waters again flows unvexed to the sea." He also sent Grant a letter of congratulations and told him that he had feared Grant's plan would fail, but "I now wish to make the personal acknowledgment that you were right, and I was wrong." With the Mississippi River completely in Union hands, the Confederacy was cut in two, and Union commerce could flow all the way from the Ohio River to New Orleans unencumbered.

When considering court-martial cases after the Gettysburg and Vicksburg campaigns, Lincoln was reluctant to approve the death penalty for

cowardice. He had made it a policy throughout the war to try to personally review every court-martial case that had resulted in a Union soldier
being sentenced to death. His hope in these reviews was to find some
"excuse" to pardon them, and this he often did—in spite of Secretary
Stanton's complaints that it undermined military discipline. Lincoln
always wondered whether or not he himself, placed in the same situation as the soldiers, would run away. In jest, he said that his reason for
pardoning the deserters was that it would "frighten the poor devils too
terribly to shoot them."

With the victories at Gettysburg and Vicksburg, the Union's military
position was significantly improved by midsummer of 1863. Lee's army
was greatly reduced in strength, and the loss of Vicksburg isolated the
Confederate states west of the Mississippi River from those to the east. In
spite of this, the Northern press and the civilian population were still in
turmoil over political issues that were being skillfully exploited by the Peace
Democrats. Among these issues were Lincoln's suspension of the writ of
habeas corpus, the national draft, and rioting in New York City over racial
issues. Peace Democrats were at the height of their political influence in
the summer of 1863, and the Democratic Party boldly nominated some
of the most radical of the Copperheads for office, including the banished
Clement Vallandigham of Ohio.

Although Grant had won a significant victory at Vicksburg, Lincoln's
army commander in eastern Tennessee, William S. Rosecrans, was having

less success. Rosecrans had initially done well, pushing General Bragg out of central Tennessee at the Battle of Stones River in early January and taking Chattanooga on August 21. But Rosecrans was unaware that while he was in Chattanooga, his opponent, Bragg, had been reinforced. General Longstreet and a force of twenty thousand men from the Army of Northern Virginia had been brought westward by railway to help Bragg.

After he refit and reequipped his army, Rosecrans marched out of Chattanooga southward toward Atlanta. But he was attacked by Bragg and Longstreet on September 19. This bitter, two-day battle, which would be known as the Battle of Chickamauga, resulted in almost thirty-five thousand casualties. On the second day of battle, Rosecrans's right wing collapsed, so he and half of his army skedaddled back to Chattanooga. But the other half of Rosecrans's army, commanded by Union general George H. Thomas, held firm against repeated attacks by the Confederates. Late in the day, Thomas performed an orderly retreat to Chattanooga and joined Rosecrans. Bragg followed Thomas and bottled up the Yankees by occupying the high ground around the city.

Rosecrans, who sent conflicting messages to Washington about the strength of his military position in Chattanooga, seemed, according to Lincoln, "confused and stunned like a duck hit on the head." Lincoln ordered Stanton to detach General Hooker and fifteen thousand troops from the Army of the Potomac and send them west by rail to reinforce Rosecrans in Chattanooga. In mid-October, Lincoln placed Grant in command of all Union armies between the Appalachian Mountains and the Mississippi River. Grant immediately fired Rosecrans, ordered General Sherman to march to Chattanooga with twenty thousand men, and went to the beleaguered city to take personal command of the forces there.

In the meantime, Confederate General Longstreet marched northward from Chattanooga and attacked General Burnside at Knoxville. Lincoln worried how the former commander at Fredericksburg would do against Longstreet and was relieved when he received a message from one of Burnside's subordinates, General John Foster. The receipt of this message indicated that Union forces had not been overwhelmed, and Lincoln said the news made him think of Sallie Carter back in Illinois. When Sallie Carter heard one of her children squall, she would say, "There goes one of my young-uns, not dead yet, bless the Lord."

While the Battle of Knoxville was raging, the November election results came in, and the Democratic Party discovered that they had overplayed their hand by nominating so many Peace Democrats for office. Republicans made substantial gains almost everywhere, and Ohio soldiers, who were allowed to vote in their camps, went 95 percent Republican. The soldiers considered the Copperheads to be traitors, and Vallandigham was defeated by more than one hundred thousand votes.

★ ★ ★

Lincoln was able to have a few days respite from Washington beginning on November 18, when he traveled to Gettysburg to answer an invitation to "make a few appropriate remarks" at the dedication ceremony for the battlefield cemetery. On November 19, well-known orator Edward Everett delivered the main address, a two-hour-long peroration, which described in detail the course of the battle that had taken place there in July. After Everett finished, Lincoln rose to present the short speech he had written and revised over the course of the previous few days. His Gettysburg Address became the most famous presidential speech in American history. Between its iconic beginning of "Four score and seven years ago" and its ending with the dedication that "government of the people, by the people, and for the people shall not perish from the earth," Lincoln declared that the men who died at Gettysburg had affirmed as *truth* what was once only a *proposition* from the Declaration of Independence, "that all men are created equal."

Within four days of Lincoln's address at Gettysburg, General Grant, who had taken command at Chattanooga, launched an overwhelming attack that forced Confederate General Bragg and his army to retreat toward Atlanta. These successes—the capture of Vicksburg and rescue of the army at Chattanooga—established Grant as the Union's most accomplished military commander.

Now that the military situation in both the East and West had improved, Lincoln was able to focus increasingly on economic and political issues. Although he had become a capable military and political leader, he did not pretend to understand the details of finance and the economy. Once, when he was talking to advisors about the ambiguities of the tariff and revenue generated by it, Lincoln said:

> There is something obscure about it. It reminds me of the fellow that came into a grocery down in Menard County at Salem, where I once lived, and called for a picayune's worth of crackers; so the clerk laid them out on the counter. After sitting awhile, he said to the clerk, "I don't want these crackers. Take them, and give me a glass of cider." So the clerk put the crackers back into the box and handed the fellow the cider. After drinking, he started for the door.
>
> "Here, Bill," called out the clerk, "pay me for your cider."
>
> "Why," said Bill, "I gave you the crackers for it."
>
> "Well, then, pay me for the crackers."
>
> "But I hain't had any," responded Bill.
>
> "That's so," said the clerk. "Well, clear out! It seems to me that I've lost a picayune somehow, but I can't make it out exactly."
>
> So it is with the tariff; somebody gets the picayune, but I don't exactly understand how.

★ ★ ★

The Union army had developed a better command structure, so Lincoln became less patient with people who were asking for military promotions. In response to someone urging a friend's promotion to brigadier general, Lincoln said, "Let me tell you something about that. You are a farmer, I believe; if not, you will understand me. Suppose you had a large cattle yard full of all sorts of cattle, cows, oxen, and bulls, and you kept selling and killing your cows and oxen, taking good care of your bulls. Bye and bye you would find out you had nothing but a yard full of old bulls, good for nothing under heaven. Now it will be just so with my army if I don't stop making Brigadier Generals."

Fortunately for the president, not all of the White House visitors had favors to ask. One day, an old acquaintance of Lincoln's arrived in the president's office just as a rather obnoxious, loudmouthed officer was leaving. Lincoln told his friend, "He's the biggest liar in Washington. You can't believe a word he says. He reminds me of an old fisherman I used to know who got such a reputation for stretching the truth that he bought a pair of scales and insisted on weighing every fish in the presence of witnesses. One day a baby was born next door, and the doctor borrowed the fisherman's scales to weigh the newborn. It weighed forty-seven pounds."

THE BAD BIRD AND THE MUDSILL.

From *Frank Leslie's Illustrated Newspaper*, February 21, 1863. This cartoon illustrates the North's frustration over Lincoln and the military's failures to capture Richmond after two years of war.

Although the strain of the war had significantly aged Lincoln, he had remained remarkably healthy throughout his presidency. But in early December, Lincoln was diagnosed with varioloid, a mild form of smallpox. No doubt thinking about the endless line of ornery office seekers, he joked that it was the first time since he had been in office that he had "something now to give to everybody who calls."

By the close of 1863, Lincoln had significantly changed the character of the war. His acts of emancipating the slaves and enlisting them in the army had met with mixed reactions at first, but by December, this had become much more acceptable to most Northerners. The North was increasing in strength. Lincoln had not only secured the border states for the Union, but he had been instrumental in the admission of a new free state, West Virginia. Thanks to Stanton, the War Department was producing mountains of military supplies and efficiently transporting them to armies in the field. The navy had imposed an effective blockade of Confederate ports that was strangling the Confederacy. Lincoln's ambassador Henry Adams reported from London that the recent military victories had put "all idea of intervention" on the part of Great Britain "at an end."

The Union controlled shipping on the Mississippi River and the Confederate states west of the Mississippi were cut off from the rest of the

Confederacy. Grant had forced the surrender of two entire Confederate armies, and many of the South's coastlands were in the hands of Union forces. Everywhere Union armies took command, thousands of slaves left their masters, never to return.

Besides these military accomplishments, Lincoln signed into law the National Banking Act of 1863, which created the U.S. National Banking System. Its legacy is the present-day national banking system and resulting U.S. banking policy.

Pragmatists in the North and South recognized what Lincoln had achieved and that it was going to be a simple matter of time before the Confederacy crumbled. But the general public did not fully grasp the significance of these accomplishments. They only saw that the strategic manufacturing center of Atlanta remained uncaptured and that Jefferson Davis still ruled defiantly from the Confederate capital of Richmond, a mere one hundred miles from Washington, DC.

This lack of complete understanding on the part of the general public was largely a result of the myopic vision of the press, especially the influential eastern newspapers like Horace Greeley's *New-York Tribune*. The press kept the North's attention focused almost exclusively on the Virginia theater of the war, and as long as Richmond was unconquered, Lincoln's political situation was tenuous.

Lincoln's secretary John Hay was one of the pragmatists who saw clearly what Lincoln had accomplished. In August 1863, he wrote about Lincoln in his journal:

The Tycoon is in fine whack. I have rarely seen him more serene and busy. He is managing this war, the draft, foreign relations, and planning a reconstruction of the Union, all at once. I never knew with what tyrannous authority he rules the Cabinet, till now. The most important things he decides and there is no cavil. I am growing more and more firmly convinced that the good of the country absolutely demands that he be kept where he is until this thing is over. There is no man in the country, so wise, so gentle, and so firm. I believe the hand of God placed him where he is.

DON'T SWAP HORSES
1864

Although Lincoln's secretary John Hay thought that "the hand of God" had made Lincoln president and it was essential that he be kept in that role, the radical Republicans weren't so sure. True, they were pleased that Lincoln had issued the Emancipation Proclamation, that he had enlisted black troops, and that he would support an amendment to end slavery. But they thought he should be going much further—such as confiscating Southern slave owners' land in order to give it to freed slaves.

The radicals also thought Lincoln pardoned too many Southerners. Once, when a petitioner came to Lincoln to ask him to pardon a Confederate surgeon who had been captured, Lincoln told him that he must ask Secretary Stanton. The man said that he had not gone to Stanton, because he knew the secretary of war would get angry and refuse to consider the case. Lincoln replied:

Perhaps there is that difference between the Secretary and myself, and it recalls a story told to me by my friend Leonard Swett: "A man had a small bull terrier that could whip all the dogs of the neighborhood. The owner of a large dog that the terrier whipped asked the owner of the terrier how it happened that his little dog whipped every other dog he encountered. 'That,' said the owner of the terrier, 'is no mystery to me; your dogs and other dogs get half through a fight before they get mad; my dog is always mad.'"

Now that the 1864 presidential election year was finally here, Treasury Secretary Salmon Chase tried again to replace Lincoln as the Republican nominee for president. Ever since his failed effort to have Seward removed from the cabinet in 1862, Chase continued to watch for opportunities to discredit Lincoln's decisions as a war leader. He used his post as secretary of the treasury to build up an army of supporters through patronage, played up to the radicals in Congress, and did everything he could think of to convince Republican leadership he would be the more electable man for the presidency in 1864.

Nevertheless, when it came to political skill, Chase wasn't even in Lincoln's league. Lincoln's supporters grew disgusted with Chase's subterfuge and began to clamor for the treasury secretary's removal from office. But Lincoln saw how hard Chase was working to impress everyone, and the situation reminded the president, of course, of another story. "My [step] brother and I," he said, "were once plowing corn, I driving the horse and he holding the plow. The horse was lazy, but on one occasion he rushed across the field so that I, with my long legs, could scarcely keep pace with him. On reaching the end of the furrow, I found an enormous chin-fly fastened upon him, and knocked him off. My brother asked me what I did that for, and I told him I didn't want the old horse bitten in that way.

"'Why,' said my brother, 'that's all that made him go!'

"Now," said Lincoln, "if Mr. Chase has a Presidential chin-fly biting him, I'm not going to knock him off, if it will only make his department go."

In explaining his reluctance to fire Chase, Lincoln said:

It isn't so easy a thing to let Chase go. I am situated very much as the boy was who held the bear by the hind legs. I will tell you how it was. There was a very vicious bear which, after being some time chased by a couple of boys, turned upon his pursuers. The boldest of the two ran up and caught the bear by the hind legs, while the other climbed up into a little tree, and complacently witnessed the conflict going on beneath, between the bear and his companion. The tussle was a sharp one, and the boy, after becoming quite exhausted, cried out in alarm, "Bill, come down and help me let this darned bear go!"

Lincoln knew he needed Chase's financial skills to run the Treasury Department. Once when Chase came to Lincoln with the complaint that the war effort was costing too much, he asked the president what could be done about it. Lincoln shrugged his shoulders and then, thinking of greenbacks, joked, "Well, Mr. Secretary, I don't know, unless you give your paper mill another turn."

Although the radical Republicans preferred Chase, the majority of Republicans, the soldiers, and the Northern civilian population liked Lincoln. His honesty, sincerity, dedication, and sense of humor had endeared him to millions.

But not everyone loved the president. In an effort to undermine his popularity, the Democratic press attacked Lincoln religiously and constantly criticized his policies. On March 2, while sitting for portrait painter Francis B. Carpenter, Lincoln reacted to a newspaper attack on him with this story:

> A traveler on the frontier found himself out of his reckoning one night in a most inhospitable region. A terrific thunderstorm came up to add to his trouble. He floundered along until his horse at length gave out. The lightning afforded him the only clue to his way, but the peals of thunder were frightful. One bolt, which seemed to crash the earth beneath him, brought him to his knees. By no means a

praying man, his petition was short and to the point: "O Lord, if it is all the same to you, give us a little more light and a little less noise!"

Lincoln stuck to his plans. In early March, he ordered General Grant to Washington, promoted him to the rank of lieutenant general, and put him in command of all Union armies. Grant appointed General Sherman commander of the Division of the Mississippi and placed him at the head of his old army in northern Georgia.

After Grant took command, he decided he would campaign with the Army of the Potomac instead of sitting at a desk in Washington, so he could make certain General Meade and his army kept constant pressure on General Lee's Army of Northern Virginia.

Lincoln and Grant discussed war strategy, and the president was delighted to find that he and his new army commander saw eye to eye on many issues. They agreed that the North had sufficient resources to overwhelm the South if it applied steady pressure. Lincoln, after hearing Grant's plans to use five separate armies concurrently, thought of the analogy of hunters preparing game and observed, "Those not skinning can hold a leg."

The more Lincoln got to know Grant, the more visibly relieved he was to have him in command. Friends visiting Lincoln in the White House commented on his excellent spirits. "Oh, yes!" he replied. "I feel better, for now I'm like the man who was blown up on a steamboat and said, on coming down, 'It makes no difference to me; I'm only a passenger!'"

Lincoln also met with General Philip Sheridan, whom Grant had brought with him from the west to take over the Army of the Potomac's cavalry corps. Like Grant, Sheridan was a small man but a hard fighter who was always at the head of the charge on the battlefield. According to Sheridan, Lincoln concluded their interview by quoting in jest "that stale interrogation so prevalent during the early years of the war, 'Who ever saw a dead cavalryman?'" The cantankerous Sheridan may have laughed at Lincoln's old joke, but he was probably not amused. He meant to use the cavalry for some hard fighting.

Grant and the Army of the Potomac headed south in early May and for months slugged it out with Lee and the Army of Northern Virginia. Grant kept attacking Lee, then moving to the southeast and attacking again. It was a terrible war of attrition, one that, as long as the North was willing to keep sending troops into the fray, the South would eventually lose. Although Lincoln was glad to have a general who didn't retreat after battle, he suffered terrible personal strain as the casualty lists grew longer and longer.

The battles in Virginia in 1864 came in rapid succession: the Wilderness, Spotsylvania Courthouse, and North Anna in May, and Cold

Harbor in June. Finally, Grant broke away from Lee and crossed the James River southeast of Richmond. He approached the strategic rail center of Petersburg, south of Richmond, in mid-June. From there, he threatened to cut off the Confederate capital from its supply lines, but Lee got to Petersburg in the nick of time and the armies began digging in, preparing for trench warfare.

At the same time Grant and Lee began fighting in Virginia, General Sherman left Chattanooga and headed his powerful army southward toward Atlanta, about one hundred miles away. Opposing Sherman's army of almost one hundred thousand was a Confederate army of fifty thousand, headed by General Joseph Johnston, who had replaced Bragg. Sherman was an experienced army commander who used his superior resources to repeatedly outflank his adversary and keep moving south. Johnston was a capable general as well, who knew how to take advantage of terrain and fight effectively on the defensive. Johnston had the advantage in that he was fighting in terrain that lent itself well to defense, so Sherman's progress was slow. It would be months before the Atlanta campaign was over.

Meanwhile, the 1864 Republican Presidential Convention assembled in Baltimore on June 7. Andrew Johnson, who had been the Democratic pro-Union governor of Tennessee, replaced Republican Hannibal Hamlin as vice-presidential running mate. Lincoln was nominated for reelection, and per the president's request, support for an amendment abolishing slavery was added to the party platform. After hearing news of his nomination, Lincoln was relieved that his party would give him a chance to finish the war and replied, "I have not permitted myself, gentlemen, to conclude that I am the best man in the country; but I am reminded, in this connection, of the story of an old Dutch farmer, who remarked to a companion once that 'it was not best to swap horses when crossing streams.'"

Later in June, Chase threatened to resign if Lincoln did not agree to a patronage appointment he had requested, a tactic he had used with Lincoln many times. But this time, instead of acceding to Chase's demands, on June 30, Lincoln shocked the treasury secretary by accepting his resignation. On July 1, Lincoln recommended the brilliant William Pitt Fessenden of Maine to take Chase's place, and the Senate immediately confirmed him. Fessenden accepted the position on July 5.

On the battlefield, the casualty lists from the Army of the Potomac in the summer of 1864 continued to climb, and this sent Lincoln into bouts of depression that even his sense of humor could not pull him out of. While in Washington, the Lincolns attended the New York Avenue Presbyterian Church with some regularity, and visitors frequently found him reading the Bible. Lincoln's thoughts and conversations at this time demonstrated that he was deeply pondering God's purpose for the war, as is evidenced by this personal meditation: "The purposes of the Almighty are perfect, and must prevail, though we erring mortals may fail to accurately perceive them in advance. We hoped for a happy termination of this terrible war long before this; but God knows best, and has ruled otherwise."

In the summer of 1864, Lincoln was visited by his old friend Joshua Speed, who found the president reading the Bible. Speed, probably thinking of Lincoln's religious skepticism in Illinois, admitted that he himself was still a religious cynic. But Lincoln had changed, and he replied, "You are wrong, Speed. Take all of this book upon reason that you can, and the balance on faith, and you will live and die a happier and better man."

On another day, while Speed was meeting with Lincoln, a delegation from the Ohio Valley states called on the president with a list of complaints and demands. Lincoln listened to them patiently, then responded with a story about a family who never stayed very long in one place: "The chickens of the family got so used to being moved that whenever they saw the wagon sheets brought out, they laid themselves on their backs and crossed their legs, ready to be tied. Now, gentlemen, if I were to listen to every committee that comes in that door, I had just as well cross my hands and let you tie me."

By mid-July, Sherman had maneuvered Confederate General Johnston's army southward to the Chattahoochee River near Atlanta. Frustrated by

Johnston's constant retreating, Confederate president Jefferson Davis decided to replace him with a much more aggressive commander, the one-armed General John Bell Hood. Hood began a series of reckless attacks on Sherman, none of which succeeded. Hood then fell back into the entrenchments that surrounded Atlanta and waited for further attacks by Sherman.

With Sherman stalled in front of Atlanta and Grant stalled outside of Richmond, Lincoln was again challenged by the Peace Democrats. They repeated their claim that the war could not be won and that the South should be allowed to secede. The Democratic Party, with an eye toward the November presidential election, chose General George B. McClellan as their candidate. Lincoln became convinced that unless there was a major war victory, he would be defeated by McClellan in November.

The requisite victory occurred at Atlanta, Georgia. Rather than attacking Atlanta directly, as Hood had hoped, Sherman began to extend his lines, slowly enveloping the city. Hood finally realized that his position was becoming untenable and suddenly withdrew his army from Atlanta on September 1. Sherman moved his army into Atlanta on September 2 and telegraphed Washington the curt message, "Atlanta is ours, and fairly won."

With this news, the political winds changed overnight. Newspapers trumpeted Atlanta's capture, and the North rejoiced. Lincoln and the Republican Party were in favor again. People saw light at the end of the tunnel, and Lincoln's reelection to the presidency was assured.

Meanwhile, in the eastern theater, General Sheridan had made a strategic march through the Shenandoah Valley, destroying Southern farmers' crops as he went. It may have been one of those farmers who complained to Lincoln that Union soldiers, in passing his farm, had helped themselves not only to hay, but to his horse also, and he hoped the president would urge the appropriate officer to consider his claim immediately. Lincoln said that this complaint reminded him of a story about an old acquaintance of his, Jack Chase, a lumberman on the Illinois River:

> Jack was a steady, sober man, and the best raftsman on the river. It was quite a trick to take the logs over the rapids; but he was skillful with a raft, and always kept her straight in the channel. Finally a steamer was put on, and Jack was made captain of her. Jack would always take the wheel going through the rapids. One day when the boat was plunging and wallowing along the boiling current, Jack's utmost vigilance was being exercised to keep her in the narrow channel. Suddenly, a boy pulled his coat-tail and hailed him with: "Say, Mister Captain! I wish you would just stop your boat a minute—I've lost my apple overboard!"

In the upcoming November election, Lincoln knew his most enthusiastic supporters would be the soldiers themselves. The men loved Lincoln and called him "Father Abraham" and "Uncle Abe." They didn't care if he wasn't dignified or presidential looking—they knew that he cared for them and he was resolute in the Union cause. When he was invited to review the troops and rode by on horseback in his ungainly way, they spontaneously broke out into cheers. Lincoln, in return, loved the soldiers and always relished talking to and encouraging them. His visits to the army in the field were something he truly enjoyed.

Lincoln won the presidential election of 1864 by a landslide. He had a popular majority of more than four hundred thousand votes in the Northern states and carried all but three states. In the Electoral College, he defeated McClellan 212 to 21, and nearly 80 percent of the soldier vote went for Lincoln.[1] Lincoln believed that the Northern people had vindicated his emancipation policy and that his plea for the people to "re-adopt the Declaration of Independence" was finally being heard.

With the election behind him, Lincoln could breathe easier, and in moments of repose he enjoyed telling stories just for the fun of it. Once he talked about the boy who, when asked how many legs his calf would have if he called the tail a leg, replied "five." But the answer was four, said Lincoln. "Calling a tail a leg would not make it a leg."

He also told a story about a couple of labor-seeking emigrants fresh from Ireland who were making their way toward the West.

---

1. For 1864 election results, see Gienapp, *Abraham Lincoln and Civil War America*, 174.

This *Frank Leslie's Budget of Fun* cartoon celebrates Republican Abraham Lincoln's reelection as president. The "Giant Majority" carrying him to victory consisted of 212 Electoral College votes to McClellan's 21.

"Coming suddenly one evening upon a pond of water, they were greeted with a grand chorus of bullfrogs, a kind of music they had never before heard: 'B-a-u-m! B-a-u-m!' Overcome with terror, they clutched their shillelaghs and crept cautiously forward, straining their eyes in every direction to catch a glimpse of the enemy, but he was not to be found. At last a happy idea seized the foremost one; he sprang to his companion and exclaimed, 'And sure, Jamie, it is my opinion it's nothing but a noise.'"

Lincoln liked to tell the story of the "witty Irish soldier, who was always boasting of his bravery when no danger was near, but who invariably retreated without orders at the first charge of an engagement. Being asked by his Captain why he did so, replied: 'Captain, I have as brave a heart as Julius Caesar ever had; but somehow or other, whenever danger approaches, my cowardly legs run away with it.'"

The war in the western theater entered a new phase. While Grant held on at Petersburg "with a bulldog grip," Sherman prepared to take about half of his army for a march across Georgia to Savannah. The rest of the army he placed under the command of General George H. Thomas and sent it back to a defensive position in Tennessee.

On November 16, Sherman broke off communications with the North and marched eastward from Atlanta with sixty thousand men. Virtually unopposed, he cut a swath of destruction sixty miles wide across the state of Georgia, destroying or consuming Southern produce and livestock along the way. Finally, Sherman and his army turned up in Savannah, Georgia. On December 22, he sent a telegram to Lincoln, offering the city as a "Christmas present."

Confederate General Hood, meanwhile, decided not to pursue Sherman and instead marched northward to fight Union General Thomas's army in Tennessee. At Nashville, on December 15, Thomas launched an overwhelming attack on the Confederates and almost completely annihilated Hood's army. Confederate military power east of the Mississippi was now reduced to Lee's weakened army facing Grant and a few thousand troops under General Johnston, opposing Sherman.

Hearing the news of Hood's army being scattered into fragments, President Lincoln told his listeners that it made him think of Bill Sykes's dog back in Illinois:

Bill Sykes had a long, yaller dog that was forever getting into his neighbors' meat houses and chicken coops. They had tried to kill it a hundred times, but the dog was always too smart for 'em. Finally, one of them got the bladder of a coon, and filled it up with powder, tying the neck around a piece of punk. When he saw the dog coming he fired the punk, split open a hot biscuit and put the bladder in. He buttered the biscuit all nicely and threw it out. The dog swallowed it at a gulp. Pretty soon there was an explosion. The head of the dog lit on the porch, the fore-legs caught astraddle the fence, the hind-legs fell in the ditch, and the rest of the dog lay around loose. Pretty soon Bill Sykes came along, and the neighbor said: "Bill I guess there ain't much of that dog of your'n left."

"Well, no," said Bill; "I see plenty of pieces, but I guess that dog, as a dog, ain't of much more account."

"Just so," Lincoln said, "there may be fragments of Hood's army around, but I guess that dog, as a dog, ain't of much more account."

Thanks to finally having competent military commanders in Grant and Sherman, Lincoln was able to focus increasingly on political issues. In October, Supreme Court justice Roger Taney had died. Worried about the courts overturning the Emancipation Proclamation when the war was over, Lincoln decided to appoint former secretary of the treasury Salmon P. Chase as chief justice of the U.S. Supreme Court. Although he recognized that Chase had been more of an enemy than a friend, he knew that in his former cabinet member, he had a reliable ally on the emancipation issue.

The year 1864 had been profitable for the Union. Unlike the South, which the war was weakening every day, the North was growing stronger. In his annual message to Congress, delivered on December 6, Lincoln was able to report details of the North's increasing strength and wealth in the midst of civil war. Toward the close of the address, he said, "The important fact remains demonstrated that we have more men now than we had when the war began; that we are not exhausted nor in process of exhaustion; that we are gaining strength and may if need be maintain the contest indefinitely. This as to men. Material resources are now more complete and abundant than ever. The national resources, then, are unexhausted, and, as we believe, inexhaustible."

With military victory now only a matter of time, the rail-splitter-turned-statesman from Illinois intended to focus his efforts in his second term on the constitutional amendment to abolish slavery, the restoration of peace, and reconstruction.

LET 'EM UP EASY
1865

A t the beginning of 1865, Lincoln's first priority was to pass the Thirteenth Amendment to the Constitution and begin the legal abolishment of slavery in the United States of America. On April 8 of the previous year, the Senate had passed the Thirteenth Amendment by the required two-thirds majority. But in the House of Representatives, where Republicans had a smaller majority, the passage of the amendment had fallen thirteen votes short. In the November election of 1864, the Republican Party had picked up sufficient votes in the House and consequently would be able to easily pass the Thirteenth Amendment when the lame-duck Congress was replaced. Unfortunately, the new Congress would not be seated until a year after the election—in December 1865.

Lincoln's concerns were that the war would end long before the new Congress was seated, he would lose the extraordinary political power he had as president during wartime, and the courts would force the freed slaves back into slavery. In Lincoln's eyes, the Northern people, in reelecting him by a four-hundred-thousand-vote majority, had vindicated his policies and accepted the proposed emancipation of the slaves. Consequently, Lincoln decided to press for passage of the amendment before the war ended, which would likely be within months.

There were two main obstacles to the immediate passage of the Thirteenth Amendment. First, the lame-duck House of Representatives had too many Democrats—the same Democrats who had almost unanimously voted against the antislavery amendment the last time. Second, the Republican leadership thought it would be much easier to pass when the next Congress was seated in December and were willing to wait.

Although Lincoln rarely interfered with House legislation, he decided to have the Thirteenth Amendment introduced in early January and brought to a vote before February 1. But the big question was how to win the lame-duck Democrats' votes. The most influential tool Lincoln had at his disposal was the patronage that he, as president, could legally hand out in any way he saw fit. Normally, of course, presidents gave patronage jobs to men of their own political party. Lincoln decided to try to influence lame-duck House Democrats by appealing to the moral values of those who could be persuaded in this way and to offer patronage jobs to those who could not be. If he could convince about twenty Democrats and border state conservatives to switch their votes, the Thirteenth Amendment would pass.

In the end, Lincoln's strategy worked. The Republican Party voted unanimously in favor of black freedom, along with sixteen Democrats, giving

Lincoln the majority he needed. He signed the Thirteenth Amendment, eliminating slavery, on February 1, and the North rejoiced. The amendment would eventually be ratified at the end of 1865 by a sufficient number of states—including two Southern states—to be signed into law.[1]

Significantly, Lincoln's Illinois, the state that in 1848 had passed a law prohibiting the settlement of free black people within its borders, was the first state to ratify the Thirteenth Amendment.

Within days of signing the amendment, Lincoln and Seward met with Confederate peace commissioners at Hampton Roads, Virginia. The commissioners were sent by Jefferson Davis to seek a peace agreement and included Vice President Alexander H. Stephens, Assistant Secretary of War John A. Campbell, and Senator R. M. T. Hunter, the former secretary of state for the Confederacy.

Lincoln was particularly glad to see Stephens, whom he had worked with in Congress seventeen years earlier. As Stephens, who was a small man, began to remove his heavy overcoat and large scarf, the president chided him: "Now, gentlemen, you see what a large amount of 'shuck' Mr. Stephens has—just wait a minute and you will be surprised to find what a small 'nubbin' he is."

---

1. For Lincoln's political maneuvers to pass the Thirteenth Amendment, see Burlingame, *Abraham Lincoln: A Life*, 2:745–50.

THE PEACE COMMISSION.
Flying to ABRAHAM'S Bosom.

This February 18, 1865, cartoon from *Harper's Weekly* depicts an enthusiastic Lincoln welcoming the Confederate Peace Commissioners who were "flying to Abraham's bosom."

They all laughed heartily and Stephens retorted with a joke about how, after first meeting Lincoln and other representatives from the Prairie State years ago, he thought Illinois should have been called "All noise."

At last, they settled down to business. Lincoln insisted on emancipation and an immediate return of the Confederate states to the Union as terms for peace. The Confederate commissioners insisted on maintaining their status as a "separate nation" and proposed instead that hostilities be suspended until they worked out the remaining terms. Attempting to justify this approach, Confederate representative Hunter argued that, historically, executives had been known to enter into agreements with parties who remained in arms against public authority. He smugly pointed to the example of Charles I of England. Lincoln shrewdly replied, "I do not profess to be posted in history. On all such matters I will turn you over to Seward. All I distinctly recollect about the case of Charles the First is that he lost his head in the end."

After a discussion on various subordinate issues, the commissioners refused to accept reunion, saying indignantly that this would be "unconditional submission," and within five hours of its beginning, the peace conference ended.

Soon after the peace conference, Lincoln and Seward decided to bolster morale by reviewing Union troops near the Petersburg front. While riding, Seward's horse became startled and then bolted toward enemy lines, taking the secretary of state and his high hat with him. Lincoln, who had watched this adventure with some amusement, said afterward, "I'm glad that horse did not make it necessary for me to make an application to the General of the Confederate army for an exchange of prisoners for a United States senator, as we have never captured any Confederate senators."

The end of the war was drawing near. The Confederacy had suffered military defeat after defeat. On January 15, Union forces captured Fort Fisher and closed the South's last major port at Wilmington, North Carolina. Sherman had marched virtually unopposed from Savannah, Georgia, through South Carolina, inflicting more than the usual amount of destruction on his way. Grant continued to extend his lines to his left at Petersburg, wrapping around Lee's increasingly thin lines and threatening the Southside Railroad—a major supply line to Richmond. Confederate soldiers, seeing the writing on the wall, deserted at an increasing rate, making their way home in order to aid their families.

Although the end of the war was approaching, every day brought more casualties, and the strain on Lincoln increased. He had never taken an extended absence from Washington, other than to visit the Army of the Potomac in the field and his trip to the dedication ceremony at Gettysburg. Occasionally for relaxation, he would take Mary to the theater to see a comedy or, his favorite, Shakespeare. He found comfort in the Bible, which he read frequently, and also enjoyed reading the works of various contemporary humorists with pseudonyms such as Artemus Ward, Petroleum V. Nasby, and Orpheus C. Kerr (Office Seeker).

The Orpheus C. Kerr papers were the sort of humor Lincoln

loved—broad exaggerations, satire, and absurd statements about the hero's life and experiences in Washington during the Civil War. Orpheus C. Kerr (whose real name was Robert Henry Newell) opened with "Though you find me in Washington now, I was born of respectable parents." Kerr frequently poked fun at Lincoln and his policies, such as his account of himself and some friends catching some chickens and deciding to "cook and eat them immediately, lest the president should administer the oath of allegiance" and let the chickens go free. Lincoln said that anyone who hadn't read the Orpheus C. Kerr papers was "a heathen."

Because of his increased need for both information and leisure, Lincoln's trips to the War Department's telegraph office became more frequent toward the end of the war. One of the clerks said that after arriving one evening and taking up a stack of telegrams to review, Lincoln read a memorandum and jocularly commented on an officer's signature that had been partly obscured by the flourish with which it ended. Lincoln said, "That reminds me of a short-legged man in a big overcoat, the tail of which was so long it wiped out his footprints in the snow."

On another trip to the telegraph office, an operator said Lincoln remarked that "he had just been reading a little book which someone had given to his son Tad. It was a story of a motherly hen who was struggling to raise her brood and teach them to lead honest and useful lives, but in her efforts she was greatly annoyed by a mischievous fox who made sad havoc with her offspring. 'I thought I would turn over to the finish and see how it came out,' said the president. 'This is what it said: "and the fox became a good fox, and was appointed paymaster in the army. I wonder who he is!"'"

The telegraph operators enjoyed Lincoln's visits and the stories he told, which eased wartime tensions. Another lighthearted tale Lincoln shared was about "a man, apparently struggling with the effects of bad whisky, [who] thrust his head out of the window and shouted loudly, 'Hullo! Hullo!'

"[A] traveler stopped and asked what was wanted. 'Nothing of *you*,' was the reply.

"'Well, what in the devil do you shout "hullo" for when people are passing?' angrily asked the traveler.

"'Well, what in the devil are you passing for when people are shouting hullo?' replied the drunk."

Inauguration Day, March 4, 1865, finally arrived—overcast and drizzly. Andrew Johnson, who had apparently taken one drink too many to calm his nerves, slurred his way through his acceptance speech and took the vice-presidential oath of office indoors. Fortunately, after this inauspicious beginning, the weather improved, and it was decided to hold the president's inauguration outside.

When Lincoln stepped up to the podium, the sun broke through the clouds and bathed the audience in light. Lincoln then presented what has been widely acclaimed as the best of all presidential inaugural speeches. In only 701 words, Lincoln articulated his meditations of the last four years about divine providence and God's purpose for the war. With allusions to seven passages of the Bible, its cadence and language was worthy of the prose of an Old Testament prophet.

Lincoln held that everyone knew it was the nation's differences over slavery that were "somehow the cause of the war." He said that both North and South thought they had acted in accordance with the will of God, because both had "read the same Bible, and invoked His aid against the other." But Lincoln, after a lifetime of reading the Bible and four years of leading millions through a terrible confrontation, had concluded that *no one* knew the mind of God in the great conflict—because "the Almighty has His own purposes." Nevertheless, the president offered his own theory about God's reason for the war. This was that the Lord, whose "judgments are true and righteous altogether," had allowed it to come as punishment for the nation's perpetuation of slavery, which had "continued through His appointed time."

Finally, looking toward the future, Lincoln pronounced his unforgettable conclusion: "With malice toward none, with charity for all, with firmness in the right as God gives us to see the right, let us strive on to finish the work we are in, to bind up the nation's wounds, to care for him who shall have borne the battle and for his widow and his orphan, to do all which may achieve and cherish a just and lasting peace among ourselves and with all nations."

At the White House reception that evening, Lincoln wanted to hear his friend Frederick Douglass's opinion of the speech. But Douglass, unknown to the president, had been prevented from entering the White House by Washington policemen because of his race. This was soon cleared up, and when Douglass appeared in the receiving line, Lincoln said loudly, "Here comes my friend Douglass!" Shaking the former slave's hand, he said, "There is no man's opinion I value more than yours; what do you think of it?" Douglass replied that he believed it to have been "a sacred effort," which pleased the president very much. Lincoln had feared men would "not [be] flattered by being shown there has been a difference of purpose between the Almighty and them."

After the inaugural ceremonies were over, Lincoln decided to visit the army. In mid-March, Lincoln took Mary and Tad on a visit to Grant's headquarters at City Point, Virginia. This outing not only allowed him to convene important meetings with Grant, Sherman, and Admiral David Porter, but it also gave the Lincolns an opportunity to see their son Robert, who was now a captain on Grant's staff. In discussing the military situation with Grant, Sherman, and Porter, Lincoln expressed his desire to let the Confederate soldiers go home immediately after they surrendered. Lincoln wanted a generous peace and hinted that he wouldn't mind if Davis and his cabinet somehow managed to successfully escape the country.

While he was visiting Grant at City Point, the general showed Lincoln the Dutch Gap Canal, where a rather grandiose Union army effort had ended in failure. Union forces had attempted to cut off a curl in the James River that was under the control of Confederate forces by digging a canal at the bend. Upon seeing the abandoned ditch, Lincoln launched into a story about a blacksmith back in Springfield, Illinois. Starting off with a large piece of soft iron, he decided to forge a farm implement out of it. Failing in that, he decided to make something smaller, a claw hammer. Failing in that, he decided to make something smaller still, an ax head. At last, he failed in that too. So, picking up the small, red-hot piece of iron with his tongs, he plunged it into the water, saying, "Well, if I can't make anything else of you, I will make a fizzle, anyhow!"

While Lincoln was reviewing troops at City Point, Mary overreacted when she saw another woman riding alongside her husband and had a temper tantrum that embarrassed not only Lincoln, but all others nearby, including Grant's wife Julia. Much to everyone's relief, Mary returned to Washington earlier than planned. Believing that the end of the war was near, Lincoln decided to keep Tad with him and stay at Grant's headquarters.

On April 1, a Union force under General Sheridan attacked Confederate general George Pickett's troops on the extreme right of Lee's army, inflicting significant casualties and threatening Lee's supply line. As a result, Lee concluded it was time to abandon Petersburg and Richmond, which he started doing the next day. Union troops entered Richmond on April 3, and the following day, Lincoln decided to visit the former capital of the Confederacy. He took a ship up the James River, but it was so large that his party soon had to transfer to a barge and then to a Captain's gig. Lincoln said to Admiral Porter, "Admiral, this [journey] brings to my mind a fellow who once came to me to ask for an appointment as minister abroad. Next, he asked to be made a tide-waiter. When he saw that he could not get that, he asked me for an old pair of trousers. It is well to be humble."

After he arrived on the dock, the victorious president walked hand in hand with his son Tad through the streets of Richmond, protected only by a small escort of sailors. Although the white residents avoided Lincoln, the city's former slaves followed him jubilantly through town. They walked through charred ruins, because much of the city had been destroyed in a fire set by evacuating Confederate troops. After a two-mile journey, they arrived at the former Confederate White House, where Lincoln and Tad went inside. Then the president sat down in an office chair and quietly remarked, "This must have been Jefferson Davis's desk." He asked for a drink of water, and when the Union general in charge of Richmond inquired how to treat its citizens, Lincoln replied, "If I were in your place, I'd let 'em up easy. Let 'em up easy."

Meanwhile, Lee's army was retreating westward as rapidly as possible, hoping to reach Danville, Virginia, for a brief rest and then to combine forces with General Johnston in North Carolina. At the Battle of Sayler's Creek, however, Union General Sheridan's forces captured a large contingent of Lee's army and then telegraphed Grant, "If the thing is pressed

I think that Lee will surrender." Reading this message, Lincoln quickly responded, "Let the thing be pressed."

Lincoln heard that Secretary Seward had been injured in a carriage accident, so he decided he would return to Washington. But before he left, the president went to the army hospital at City Point and personally greeted several thousand Union and Confederate soldiers. One surprised onlooker said that he was just as kind and considerate to the wounded Confederate soldiers as he was to those from the Union army.

Shortly after this visit, Lincoln noticed two fire axes hanging on a wall and said, "'Well, now, I wonder if I could lift one of those axes up by the end of the handle.' He proceeded to do so, holding it at arm's length for several seconds, after which he said: 'When I used to split rails, thirty years ago in Illinois, I could lift two axes that way, and I believe I could do it now, and I will try it some other time.'" After Lincoln left, some of the soldiers tried repeating the same feat but couldn't do it.

Lincoln returned to Washington via river boat, and while in transit, he read passages of Shakespeare to his guests on the *River Queen*. After hours of relaxation with *Hamlet*, he arrived late in the afternoon of April 9. That evening, he received a telegram from Grant, saying that Lee had surrendered the Army of Northern Virginia on terms "proposed by myself." Although there were still Confederate armies in North Carolina and west of the Mississippi River that had not yet surrendered, the nightmare of war for Lincoln—as well as the rest of the country—was finally over.

After the firing of five hundred cannon announced Lee's surrender in Washington the next day, the city broke into a noisy celebration of bells ringing, people cheering, and bands playing. That evening, a crowd stood on the White House lawn, singing songs and calling for Lincoln to speak, which he finally did from the balcony. He limited his speech to a few brief remarks and promised to deliver a longer speech the following evening. In departing, he surprised everyone when he asked the band to play "one of the best tunes" he had ever heard, "Dixie."

The next evening, the crowd returned, and Lincoln read his address. Although the audience expected a speech of acclamation and triumph, Lincoln's mind was focused instead on the problem of Reconstruction and readmittance of the Southern states to the Union. He suggested that some black men, such as former soldiers, be allowed to vote. Listening in the audience was the well-known actor John Wilkes Booth, a Southern partisan who had been plotting to kidnap Lincoln and deliver him to the Confederacy. When he heard the part about former slaves being allowed to vote, he was incensed and purportedly swore, "That is the last speech he will ever make."

If he actually made that pledge, Booth's boast was not in vain. Although Secretary Stanton and Lincoln's friend Ward Hill Lamon, who was marshal of the District of Columbia, had done their best to protect the president from would-be assassins during the war, Lincoln had always believed that anyone truly intent on killing him would be able to succeed in spite of bodyguards. He abhorred the idea of the leader of a free people being surrounded by guards and took very few personal precautions for his own safety.

On Good Friday, April 14, Lincoln invited a special guest to his cabinet meeting. Per Lincoln's request, General Grant came to share details about the last few days of the war. The president, who according to cabinet members was in "a grand mood," took the opportunity to talk again about his desire for a generous peace with the South. He talked about Reconstruction and how he was glad that Congress was no longer in session so that he could have a few Southern state governments in place before Congress convened in December.

When asked about what to do with Jefferson Davis and other prominent leaders of the Confederacy, Lincoln gestured with his hands as if he were shooing chickens across the barnyard and suggested that "they frighten them out of the country." He disavowed any personal feelings of vindictiveness and said that he thought "enough lives had been sacrificed."

Lincoln described to his cabinet a dream he had had the preceding night, in which he said that he seemed to be in some "singular, indescribable vessel," and that he "was moving with great rapidity." He said he had also had this dream preceding Fort Sumter, Bull Run, Antietam, Gettysburg, Stones River, Vicksburg, and Wilmington. He expressed his belief, based on these previous dreams, they would have "some great news very soon."

There are other testimonies of Lincoln's generous attitude toward

Confederate leaders in his last days. Grant said that Lincoln illustrated his point of hoping Confederate leaders would "accidentally" get away by telling the joke about the Irishman who, having to swear off liquor for health reasons, held his glass of soda water behind him and said: "Doctor, couldn't you drop a bit of brandy in that, unbeknownst to meself?" Charles A. Dana asked the president whether they should arrest a Confederacy's agent who had been discovered within Union lines, and Lincoln replied: "Well, no, I rather think not. When you have got an elephant on hand, and he's trying to run away, it's best to let him run."

Later that day, he and Mary took a carriage ride. He was in a happy mood now and seemed more relaxed than he had been for a long time. "Mary later recalled that she said to him 'Dear husband you almost startle me by your great cheerfulness.'"

Lincoln responded, "And well I may feel so, Mary. I consider *this* day, the war has come to a close. We must both be more cheerful in the future. Between the war and the loss of our darling Willie—we have both been very miserable."

The Lincolns had invited General Grant and his wife Julia to attend Ford's Theatre that night to see the comedy *Our American Cousin*. But Julia asked her husband to decline. Instead of the Grants, a young couple, Major Henry Rathbone and his fiancée Clara Harris, accompanied the Lincolns. It is unfortunate that Grant did not attend, since, unlike Lincoln, he usually had a strong military bodyguard with him.

The Lincoln party arrived after the play had started and took their place in the president's special box to the upper right of the stage. The audience broke into spontaneous cheers and the band interrupted the play to perform "Hail to the Chief." Then things quieted down and the Lincolns settled in to enjoy the play. The Washington policeman who had accompanied them left his post in order to find a better place from which to watch the entertainment.

John Wilkes Booth was popular at Ford's Theatre, having been an actor there for many years, and he had no trouble convincing the White House footman that he had business with the president. He entered the presidential box and waited for an opportune moment. When the audience laughed loudly, Booth emerged from the back of the box and shot Lincoln in the back of the head with his derringer. Major Rathbone leaped up to detain him, but Booth brandished a large knife and cut him severely. Booth jumped down to the stage and broke his leg when he landed. He cried out to the stunned audience, "Sic Semper Tyrannis!" (thus always to tyrants!), the motto of the state of Virginia, before limping offstage and jumping onto his horse to escape.

The theater erupted as the audience realized that the president had been shot. Two doctors, one of whom was young Julia Taft's older brother, quickly made their way to the presidential booth. The bullet had entered Lincoln's skull from the back and was still lodged in his brain. The doctors decided to move him across the street to a private residence, and with the help of a small escort of soldiers, they managed to clear a way through the panic-stricken crowd.

His tall form was laid diagonally across a bed. Soon, his wife Mary, son Robert, and various government officials started to arrive. Seward had been attacked by one of Booth's conspirators as well and could not come to the president's side. But Stanton was there, taking charge in the midst of chaos and organizing a manhunt for the assassin, who by then had been confirmed as the actor John Wilkes Booth. The doctors realized that the president's situation was hopeless, and all that mortal man could do was to wait through the long hours of the night for the inevitable.

At 7:22 the next morning, Saturday, April 15, Abraham Lincoln breathed his last. A minister offered a short prayer, and after a poignant moment, gruff old secretary of war Edwin Stanton, choking on his tears, solemnly said, "Now he belongs to the ages."

It was a gray, overcast morning, and thousands of people in Washington had already heard the news. Hundreds waited quietly outside the house where Lincoln lay, apparently indifferent to the aroma of the blooming lilacs and the falling of a light rain. Soon the word of the president's passing began to be whispered from one person to another. Countless citizens, black and white, soldiers and civilians, rich and poor, wept openly. Then, one by one, the church bells of the city began to toll, proclaiming to the world the passing of the United States of America's greatest, and most highly esteemed, leader.

AFTERWORD
BY MICHAEL BURLINGAME

Lincoln's humor reveals aspects of his life and character that are not always fully appreciated. For example, he was an inveterate punster as well as a highly gifted teller of jokes and stories. His word play was sometimes primitive to the point of childishness. For example, one day upon seeing a store emblazoned "T. R. Strong," he allegedly remarked to his secretary of state, William Henry Seward, that "T. R. Strong but coffee are stronger." More often he demonstrated much greater verbal ingenuity. Early in the Civil War, a White House caller was discussing the Washington *States and Union*, a pro-secession newspaper that cost one cent per issue. Upon hearing its editor described as a "very penetrating man," the president quipped, "That may be, but his paper is a *penny-traitor.*"

In February 1861, while en route to Washington to assume the presidency, Lincoln stopped in New York, where he was given a reception at City Hall. When the doors opened to admit the general public, the huge number of callers burst in like water gushing from a breached reservoir. As the hordes pressed toward him, he said, "They are members of the press."

Toward the end of the conflict, Lincoln toured the war-ravaged city of Petersburg, Virginia. At a residence which Union general George L. Hartsuff had made his headquarters, that officer complained about the homeowner's demand for rent. The president gestured toward a hole in the wall caused by a Union artillery shell and remarked, "I think our batteries have given him enough rents without asking for more."

To a journalist who predicted that the newly installed Lincoln administration would be a "reign of steel," the president replied that the scandal-ridden administration of his predecessor, James Buchanan, should be called "the reign of stealing."

During the latter stages of the war, Union army recruiters offered bonuses (called bounties) to encourage volunteering. Some unscrupulous men, known as "bounty jumpers," would take the bounty, serve briefly, then desert and rejoin to receive another bounty. One day as Lincoln stood at a White House window observing a pet goat cavorting on the lawn, he told a friend, "He feeds on my bounty, and jumps with joy. Do you think we could call him a bounty jumper?"

The ability to toss off ingenious puns is a sign of linguistic intelligence, and Lincoln had an unusually high IQ, a quality that is sometimes overshadowed in the public mind by his magnanimity, eloquence, statesmanship, and benevolence.

★ ★ ★

Abundant evidence indicates that Lincoln's marriage was a difficult one, but Lincoln seldom talked about his wife to anyone. (He made an exception for his good friend Orville H. Browning, who often visited the White House during the Civil War. Browning later recalled how the president would tell him "about his domestic troubles," and that "several times he told me there that he was constantly under great apprehension lest his wife should do something which would bring him into disgrace.")

While Lincoln was usually close-mouthed about his marriage, some indication of his feelings may be gleaned from humorous quips and jokes he made about holy matrimony. Late in the war, he pardoned a young soldier who had gone AWOL in order to marry his sweetheart. Condemned to death for desertion, the prisoner became yet another beneficiary of Lincoln's legendary mercy. To one of the soldier's defenders, the president wryly observed as he signed the necessary documents, "I want to punish the young man—probably in less than a year he will wish I had withheld the pardon."

Lincoln told many jokes about henpecked husbands, with whom he evidently identified. Among them was a hapless Mr. Jones whom Lincoln described as "one of your meek men" with "the reputation of being badly henpecked." A few days after Mrs. Jones "was seen switching him out of the house," a friend told him that a "man who will stand quietly and take a switching from his wife, deserves to be horsewhipped."

Jones responded, "Why, it didn't *hurt* me any; and you've no idea what a *power* of good it did Sarah Ann!"

Lincoln was "much amused" when a friend told a story about two men who met after a long separation:

> "Where have you been, Jim?"
>
> "Oh! It was so quiet at home, I enlisted and have been in the war since I saw you—and where have you been?"
>
> "Oh! Susie made so much war on me at home that I went out timbering in the woods to get a little peace."

During the Civil War, Lincoln was asked if Clement L. Vallandigham, a Democratic critic of the administration who had been banished to the Confederacy, should be captured and tried if he returned from exile. The president replied, "Perhaps the best way to treat him would be to do as the man did who had been annoyed with a very troublesome wife, and who had been relieved by her absconding, and who by no means desired her return, and who therefore advertised *one cent* for her return."

Lincoln also told a story about a farmer who consulted him about obtaining a divorce after he and his wife had quarreled about the color to paint their new house. His client explained, "I wanted it painted white like our neighbors' houses, but my wife preferred brown. Our disputes finally became quarrels. She has broken crockery, throwing it at my head, and poured scalding tea down my back and I want a divorce." Lincoln urged the couple to compose their differences for their children's sake. Soon thereafter the farmer told Lincoln that he and his wife had reached a compromise: "We are going to paint the house brown."

As Gordon Leidner points out throughout this book, Lincoln often poked fun at himself. His self-deprecating humor was of a piece with his genuinely modest manner. (Toward the end of his life, Lincoln told a good friend, "I am very sure that if I do not go away from here [Washington] a wiser man, I shall go away a better man, for having learned here what a very poor sort of man I am.") Most politicians (indeed, most people) are dominated by their own petty egos. They take things personally, try to dominate one another, waste time and energy on feuds and vendettas, project their unacceptable qualities onto others, displace anger and rage, and put the needs of their own clamorous egos above all other considerations. A dramatic exception to this pattern, Lincoln's high degree of consciousness enabled him to suppress his own egotism while steadily focusing on the main goal: victory in the Civil War. As a friend observed, "He managed his politics upon a plan entirely different from any other man the country has ever produced…In his conduct of the war he acted upon the theory that but one thing was necessary, and that was a united North.

Abraham Lincoln, 1863

He had all shades of sentiments and opinions to deal with, and the consideration was always presented to his mind: How can I hold these discordant elements together?" In a less conscious man, envy, jealousy, self-righteousness, false pride, vanity, and the other foibles of ordinary humanity would have undermined his ability to maintain Northern unity and resolve.

Lincoln's ability to transcend his ego, as manifested in his self-deprecating humor and in other ways, was not only a key to his success as a war leader, but also forms a precious part of his legacy to the nation. He serves as a model for Americans—and all humankind—of psychological wholeness, rootedness, and maturity.

ACKNOWLEDGMENTS

I have been honored to be affiliated with one of the nation's premier organizations of scholars, the Abraham Lincoln Institute, for more than fifteen years now as a board member and webmaster. Most of the ALI's board of directors are nationally recognized experts on the subject of Abraham Lincoln, and many are also, to my good fortune, my friends. A few were able to make time in their busy schedules to review *Lincoln's Gift* and provide critical comments for improvement. They are:

Acclaimed Lincoln scholar Michael Burlingame, who not only read the manuscript and offered his advice for correction and improvement, but also, being an expert on Lincoln's humor himself, provided an insightful afterword.

Charles Hubbard, the longtime Lincoln scholar at Lincoln Memorial University of Harrogate, Tennessee. Professor Hubbard gave not only a careful reading of the manuscript, but also his passionate attention to getting the details of Lincoln's life *right*. The knowledge he has attained through his lifelong study of Abraham Lincoln has benefited thousands of students over the years as well as the readers of this book.

William C. Harris, the author of a dozen acclaimed Lincoln books and professor emeritus of history from North Carolina State University. Professor Harris likewise made excellent suggestions for the improvement of the manuscript and saved this student of Abraham Lincoln from the embarrassment of several factual errors.

Jonathan W. White, assistant professor of history at Christopher Newport University and expert on subjects such as treason in the Civil War and the effect of emancipation on the Union army. Professor White provided a careful read of the chapter on Lincoln's first year as president. He not only identified several inaccuracies, but also offered keen insight on Lincoln's difficulties during his first year in the White House.

To each of these men, I can offer no more than a sincere thank-you. In the event that any errors have slipped through in spite of these scholars' attentions, they are definitely through my own fault and not theirs.

I would also like to thank the following people and organizations for their assistance in obtaining the images and political cartoons in the book: the staff of the Prints and Photographs Room of the Library of Congress, Heather Crocetta and the staff of the Arlington County (Virginia) Public Library, Rich West of Periodyssey, Kara S. Vetter of the Indiana State Museum, and Jackie Penny of the American Antiquarian Society.

Countless thanks go to my editors at Sourcebooks, particularly Stephanie

Bowen, Ariel Bronson, and Jenna Skwarek, whose expertise in the writing and presentation of an interesting story is only surpassed by their boundless enthusiasm for their art. Special thanks as well to production editor Rachel Kahn, designer Melanie Jackson, copy editor Sabrina Baskey, and proofreader Sharon Sofinski.

And finally, "the last shall be first." My deepest thanks go to Jean, the love of my life and my wife of more than thirty-five years. Without her support, editing skills, advice, and knowledge about things like misplaced modifiers and when to use "who" and "that," this book would still be a collection of scattered papers lying on the living room floor.

A NOTE ON PRIMARY SOURCES

I used dozens of sources to assemble this short biography of Abraham Lincoln, all of which are listed in the bibliography. The following works, however, were the most invaluable:

My basic source for Lincoln's writings was *The Collected Works of Abraham Lincoln*, in eight volumes; Roy P. Basler, editor, Marion Dolores Pratt and Lloyd A. Dunlap, assistant editors, published in 1955 by the Rutgers University Press.

My three primary resources for biographical information on Lincoln were Michael Burlingame's multivolume *Abraham Lincoln: A Life*, which is today widely recognized as the definitive biography of Lincoln; David Herbert Donald's *Lincoln*, the fundamental single-volume biography; and Benjamin Thomas's *Abraham Lincoln: A Biography*, which remains the imminently readable, one-volume classic on the life of our sixteenth president.

Don E. and Virginia Fehrenbacher's *Recollected Words of Abraham*

Lincoln is invaluable for not only the breadth of its collection, but also its methodical assessment of the reliability of Lincoln "sayings" not in Basler's *Collected Works of Abraham Lincoln.* P. M. Zall's two works on Lincoln's humor provide a comprehensive collection of Lincoln's jokes and humorous stories. These are *Abe Lincoln Laughing: Humorous Anecdotes from Original Sources by and about Abraham Lincoln* and *Abe Lincoln's Legacy of Laughter: Humorous Stories by and about Abraham Lincoln.*

Essential information on Lincoln's earlier years is from Douglas Wilson and Rodney Davis's *Herndon's Informants: Letters, Interviews, and Statements about Abraham Lincoln.* Through this massive, single-volume work, the authors provide a superbly edited, complete collection of the William Herndon papers, without which the world would know little of Lincoln's early years.

Allen C. Guelzo's *Fateful Lightning: A New History of the Civil War and Reconstruction* provides not only an excellent history of the events and characters of the war, but as is typical of Guelzo, the ideas that drove them as well. James McPherson's *Battle Cry of Freedom* has long been the standard one-volume work of the events leading up to and including Civil War. Finally, *Lincoln Day by Day: A Chronology, 1809–1865* by Earl S. Miers is still the most valuable source for a detailed timeline of Lincoln's life.

NOTES

INTRODUCTION

ix   "reckon I do" Rice, *Reminiscences*, 427.

x   "Abraham is joking" Zall, *Abe Lincoln Laughing*, 151.

xi   "for any boy" Basler, *Collected Works*, 2:3.

xi   into a horse chestnut ibid., 3:16.

xi   "go it bear" ibid., 3:298.

xii   "feet get cold" McClure, *Lincoln's Yarns*, 141.

xii   "died long ago" Rice, *Reminiscences*, 442.

xii   "like the critter" Fehrenbacher and Fehrenbacher, *Recollected Words*, 270.

xii   "like a dog at a root" Thomas, *Lincoln's Humor*, 7.

xii   "a longer tail" ibid., 22.

xii   "on both sides" Fehrenbacher and Fehrenbacher, *Recollected Words*, 265.

xiii "uglier than myself" Carpenter, *Inner Life*, 148–49.

xiii   "he would die" Zall, *Abe Lincoln Laughing*, 6.

CHAPTER 1

1   "the newborn babe" Wilson and Davis, *Herndon's Informants*, 38.

1   "never come to much" ibid., 726.

2   "esteemed of my fellow men" Wilson, *Honor's Voice*, 90.

3   "moved by the stories" Wilson and Davis, *Herndon's Informants*, 37.

3   "everything and everybody" ibid., 37.

5   "reverence and worship God" ibid., 40.

5   "ragged and dirty" ibid., 41.

6   "expect to see" ibid., 108.

7   "as a wizzard" Basler, *Collected Works*, 3:511.

8   "damn three fellers" Warren, *Lincoln's Youth*, 83.

9   "down to sleep" ibid., 29.

9   "get his hands on" Wilson and Davis, *Herndon's Informants*, 107.

9   "his dog could eat the meal" Warren, *Lincoln's Youth*, 45.

9   "old hussy" Herndon and Weik, *Herndon's Lincoln*, 1:59.

9   "apparently killed" Basler, *Collected Works*, 4:62.

11   "fools to read" Basler, *Collected Works*, 1:1.

11   "darn good lies" Hertz, *Hidden Lincoln*, 8.

11   "kept the Bible" Warren, *Lincoln's Youth*, 212.

11   "pertinent quotations" Burlingame, *Abraham Lincoln: A Life*, 1:38.

11   "powerful memory" ibid., 1:21.

11   "anything he Read" Wilson and Davis, *Herndon's Informants*, 7.

11   "piece of steel" ibid., 499.

12   "cracking a joke" ibid., 37.

12   "which is wust" Warren, *Lincoln's Youth*, 194.

12   "good many short ones" Herndon and Weik, *Herndon's Lincoln*, 1:46.

13   "learned him to work" Warren, *Lincoln's Youth*, 141.

13   "neglecting his work" Wilson and Davis, *Herndon's Informants*, 41.

13   "used to be a slave" Burlingame, *Abraham Lincoln: A Life*, 1:42.

13   "soldier of the cross" Wilson and Davis, *Herndon's Informants*, 148.

13   "fighting bees" Fehrenbacher and Fehrenbacher, *Recollected Words*, 457.

14   the last hymn Warren, *Lincoln's Youth*, 121.

14   "world seemed wider and fairer" Guezlo, *Abraham Lincoln: Redeemer President*, 34.

15   "That's not so…" Burlingame, *Abraham Lincoln: A Life*, 1:32.

15   "What a fool you are" ibid.

16   muddy footprints Warren, *Lincoln's Youth*, 194.

16   "a disgrace" Burlingame, *Abraham Lincoln: A Life*, 1:53.

CHAPTER 2

19   "floating driftwood" Lamon, *Life of Abraham Lincoln*, 2:88.

19   "three nights in a row" Wilson, *Honor's Voice*, 87.

20   "make a cat laugh" Burlingame, *Abraham Lincoln: A Life*, 1:53.

20   "People relied" Wilson and Davis, *Herndon's Informants*, 386.

20   "uglier than you" McClure, *Lincoln's Yarns*, 65.

21   "turning point" Burlingame, *Abraham Lincoln: A Life*, 1:62.

22   "as big a hog" *Old Abe's Jokes*, 124.

22   "spasmodic shaking" Wilson, *Honor's Voice*, 101.

23   "swears the same" Zall, *Abe Lincoln Laughing*, 53.

24   "husband's first wife" ibid., 137.

24   "Scriptures and other" Basler, *Collected Works*, 1:5.

25   "much chagrined" Wilson, *Honor's Voice*, 90.

26   "to the Devil, sir" Herndon and Weik, *Herndon's Lincoln*, 1:94.

26   "of the gate" Hubbard, *Lincoln Reshapes the Presidency*, 10.

27   "Try me" Fehrenbacher and Fehrenbacher, *Recollected Words*, 184.

27   "Fellow citizens…" Burlingame, *Abraham Lincoln: A Life*, 1:73.

30   "respect for your eggs" Wilson and Davis, *Herndon's Informants*, 373.

30   "remain in it" Hertz, *Lincoln Talks*, 81.

33   "your eyebrow" Zall, *Abe Lincoln Laughing*, 14.

34   "bad policy" Basler, *Collected Works*, 1:75.

34   "I'm moved" Herndon and Weik, *Herndon's Lincoln*, 1:185.

34   "the only things" Burlingame, *Abraham Lincoln: A Life*, 1:97.

35   "company of women" ibid., 1:98.

36   "pleased with her" Basler, *Collected Works*, 1:117–18.

36   "made a fool of" ibid., 1:119.

36   "blockhead enough" ibid.

37   "one long step" ibid., 1:66.

37   "rule in the White House" Keckley, *Behind the Scenes*, 71.

38   "in the worst way" Burlingame, *Abraham Lincoln: A Life*, 1:175.

40   "bodder ye" Shenk, *Lincoln's Melancholy*, 118.

40   "impatient to know" Basler, *Collected Works*, 1:303.

40   "happiness would be the result" Burlingame, *Abraham Lincoln: A Life*, 1:194.

40   "To hell, I reckon" Wilson, *Honor's Voice*, 292.

41   "Statute fixes" Burlingame, *Abraham Lincoln: A Life*, 1:196.

41   "profound wonder" Basler, *Collected Works*, 1:305.

CHAPTER 3

44   "Be Crippled" Burlingame, *Abraham Lincoln: A Life*, 1:192.

44   "terrible time" ibid., 1:219.

46   "trotting harness" Hertz, *Lincoln Talks*, 110.

47   "laugh and romp" ibid., 115.

48   "scoffer at" Basler, *Collected Works*, 1:382.

49   "going to Congress" Jones, *Lincoln and the Preachers*, 44.

51   "say nothing" Basler, *Collected Works*, 1:465.

51   "hang of the school-house" Zall, *Abe Lincoln Laughing*, 142.

52   "jines [joins] mine" Lamon, *Recollections of Abraham Lincoln*, 285.

52   "Mister Speaker…gang of hogs" Basler, *Collected Works*, 1:507–16.

CHAPTER 4

55   "anywhere else" Herndon and Weik, *Herndon's Lincoln*, 2:315.

56   "new hat" ibid., 2:314.

56   "two senses" Burlingame, *Abraham Lincoln: A Life*, 1:30.

57   "with all thy soul" Wolf, *Religion of Abraham Lincoln*, 75.

58   "not domestically happy" Wilson and Davis, *Herndon's Informants*, 349.

59   "a chance dinner" Whitney, *Life on the Circuit*, 42.

60   "Why, brother Snap...too lazy to stop" ibid., 44.

61   "the keyhole" Fehrenbacher and Fehrenbacher, *Recollected Words*, 178.

62   "when they were young" Whitney, *Life on the Circuit*, 48–49.

63   "merciful Maker" Basler, *Collected Works*, 2:97.

63   "back in a ditch" Burlingame, *Abraham Lincoln: A Life*, 1:350.

63   "strongest jury lawyer" Duff, *Abraham Lincoln, Prairie Lawyer*, 190.

64   "Skin defendant" Hill, *Lincoln the Lawyer*, 216.

65   "not know him" ibid., 215.

65   "see it again" Zall, *Abe Lincoln Laughing*, 59.

66   "high-priced man" Basler, *Collected Works*, 2:333.

66   "impoverishing the bar" Hill, *Lincoln the Lawyer*, 243.

67   "end in view" Lamon, *Recollections of Abraham Lincoln*, 17.

67   "If that's Latin" Hill, *Lincoln the Lawyer*, 131.

68   "kill my dog" Zall, *Abe Lincoln Laughing*, 118–19.

68   "Why J. Parker Green?" Guelzo, *Abraham Lincoln: Redeemer President*, 86.

69   "not quite right" Hill, *Lincoln the Lawyer*, 220.

70   "was called to the door…" McClure, *Lincoln's Yarns*, 211.

70   "some other time" Holzer, *Father Abraham*, 54.

71   "what on airth" Zall, *Abe Lincoln's Legacy of Laughter*, 8.

CHAPTER 5

73   "esteemed of [his] fellow men" Wilson, *Honor's Voice*, 90.

73   "one had never lived" Gienapp, *Abraham Lincoln and Civil War America*, 48.

74   "told a little story…for the defendant" Burlingame, *Abraham Lincoln: A Life*, 1:318.

74   "old mud scow…brain failed to work" ibid., 1:351.

75   "hell of a storm" Donald, *Lincoln*, 168.

75   "[burning] effigy" Angle, *Created Equal?*, 180.

76   "always hated slavery" Basler, *Collected Works*, 2:492.

77   "dangerous opponent" Zall, *Abe Lincoln's Legacy of Laughter*, 10.

78   "re-adopt the Declaration" Basler, *Collected Works*, 2:276.

78   "injustice of slavery" ibid., 2:255.

79   "first man to discover" Burlingame, *Abraham Lincoln: A Life*, 1:378.

80   "alloy of hypocrisy" Basler, *Collected Works*, 2:323.

82   "give you my note" ibid., 2:222.

82   "stay at home" Burlingame, *Abraham Lincoln: A Life*, 1:414.

83   "perfect homogeneity" White, *Abraham Lincoln in 1854*, 11.

83   "another great man" Fehrenbacher and Fehrenbacher, *Recollected Words*, 491.

84   "tail breaks" Basler, *Collected Works*, 2:384.

85   "Wilkie can you tell me…" Burlingame, *Abraham Lincoln: A Life*, 1:221.

85   "Mary, you remind me…raised thunder amazingly" ibid.

85   "parental tyranny" ibid., 1:254.

85   "father's good-nature" Herndon and Weik, *Herndon's Lincoln*, 3:426.

86   "wring their little necks" Hertz, *Hidden Lincoln*, 105.

86   "kept [his] mouth shut" Donald, *Lincoln*, 160.

86   "bound to respect" McPherson, *Battle Cry of Freedom*, 174.

87   "pursuit of happiness" Basler, *Collected Works*, 2:405.

87   "a little engine" Donald, *Lincoln*, 81.

CHAPTER 6

90   "first and only" Burlingame, *Abraham Lincoln: A Life*, 1:458.

90   "A house divided…" Basler, *Collected Works*, 2:461–62.

91   "white men" Donald, *Lincoln*, 210.

91   "hardly won" Thomas, *Abraham Lincoln*, 182.

92   "no royalty" McClure, *Lincoln's Yarns*, 155.

93   "be overmatched" Zall, *Abe Lincoln Laughing*, 5.

93   "has the better of it" Fehrenbacher and Fehrenbacher, *Recollected Words*, 374.

95   "every living man" Basler, *Collected Works*, 3:16.

95   "Hoosier, with the gingerbread" ibid., 3:20.

95   "only a small man" ibid., 3:22.

96   "consistency of a corn-cob" ibid., 3:118.

97   "Euclid a liar" ibid., 3:186.

97   "been through college" Burlingame, *Abraham Lincoln: A Life*, 1:529.

97   "take the eels out" Basler, *Collected Works*, 3:228.

98   "shadow of a pigeon" ibid., 3:279.

98   "moral, social, and political wrong" ibid., 3:312–14.

98   "too big to cry" Burlingame, *Abraham Lincoln: A Life*, 1:548.

99   "slip and not a fall" Goodwin, *Team of Rivals*, 665.

99   "sink out of view" Basler, *Collected Works*, 3:339.

99   "if slavery is not wrong" ibid., 7:281.

99   "beat Stephen A. Douglas" Burlingame, *Abraham Lincoln: A Life*, 1:555.

100   "household purposes" Basler, *Collected Works*, 3:338.

100   "cause of civil liberty" ibid., 3:339.

101   "mighty good water" Burlingame, *Abraham Lincoln: A Life*, 1:342.

101   "This is an indictment...old man" Zall, *Abe Lincoln Laughing*, 43.

101   "concentrate more words" Fehrenbacher and Fehrenbacher, *Recollected Words*, 351.

101   "not think myself fit for the Presidency" Burlingame, *Abraham Lincoln: A Life*, 1:558.

102   "so good a time" ibid., 1:91.

103   "be a murderer" Basler, *Collected Works*, 3:547.

103   *"right makes might"* ibid., 3:550.

104   "in my mouth" Guelzo, *Abraham Lincoln: Redeemer President*, 241.

104   "back of his chair" Conwell, *Why Lincoln Laughed*, 16.

104   "fought himself out" Nicolay and Hay, *Complete Works of Lincoln*, 5:125.

106   "no bargains" Basler, *Collected Works*, 2:461.

106   "Lincoln ain't here" Fraker, *Lincoln's Ladder*, 231.

107   "Glory to God" Thomas, *Abraham Lincoln*, 214.

107   "lady over yonder" Wilson, *Lincoln among His Friends*, 137.

109   "ladies like whiskers" Basler, *Collected Works*, 4:130.

109   "silly affection" ibid., 4:129.

110   "some new clothes" Fehrenbacher and Fehrenbacher, *Recollected Words*, 296.

110   "Moses or the prophets" Hertz, *Lincoln Talks*, 171.

110   "to quiet myself" Zall, *Abe Lincoln Laughing*, 148.

111   "shall fire the Southern heart" Walther, *William Lowndes Yancey*, 222.

112   "be no compromise" Basler, *Collected Works*, 4:149.

112   "inside of the little one" Herndon and Weik, *Herndon's Lincoln*, 3:622.

113   "will see each other again" Wilson and Davis, *Herndon's Informants*, 137.

113   "go right on practicing law" Dirck, *Lincoln the Lawyer*, 151.

113   "I am decided" Wilson and Davis, *Herndon's Informants*, 685.

114   "an affectionate farewell" Basler, *Collected Works*, 4:190.

CHAPTER 7

116   "was a man…reach the capital" Fehrenbacher and Fehrenbacher, *Recollected Words*, 456.

116   "never saw him again" *Schenectady Gazette*, November 4, 1936, 17.

116   "long and the short" Basler, *Collected Works*, 4:242.

116   "foot down firmly" ibid., 4:237.

117   "not be enemies" ibid., 4:271.

119   "the best of us" Goodwin, *Team of Rivals*, 364.

120   "they must do" Basler, *Collected Works*, 4:342.

122   "that one be violated" White, *Abraham Lincoln and Treason*, 37.

123   "pleasant and kind" Bayne, *Tad Lincoln's Father*, 3.

123   "flies instead of walking" ibid., 5.

123   "tear down the White House" ibid., 43.

123   "not Pa's looking glass" ibid., 49.

124   "end to free government" Basler, *Collected Works*, 4:426.

125   "to the scaffold" Gienapp, *Abraham Lincoln and Civil War America*, 84.

126   "to die in the street" Fehrenbacher and Fehrenbacher, *Recollected Words*, 139.

127   "he would do it" McClure, *Lincoln's Yarns*, 151.

127   "bail out the Potomac" Fehrenbacher and Fehrenbacher, *Recollected Words*, 165–66.

127   "swear just like Governor" McClure, *Lincoln's Yarns*, 389.

130   "to lose Kentucky" Harris, *Lincoln and the Border States*, 3.

132   "said amen…hopeless minority" Zall, *Abe Lincoln Laughing*, 126.

132   "Well…scampered away" Hertz, *Lincoln Talks*, 356–57.

132   "God wouldn't trust 'em" Fehrenbacher and Fehrenbacher, *Recollected Words*, 436.

133   "don't want much" Gienapp, *Abraham Lincoln and Civil War America*, 91.

133   busy in letting rooms Carpenter, *Inner Life of Abraham Lincoln*, 129.

134   "sicker'n your man" McClure, *Lincoln's Yarns*, 162.

134   "steal a red hot stove" Woodburn, *Life of Thaddeus Stevens*, 600.

134   "rotten spot" Fehrenbacher and Fehrenbacher, *Recollected Words*, 217.

136   "Silver and gold" Hertz, *Lincoln Talks*, 224.

136   "better than any house" Gienapp, *Abraham Lincoln and Civil War America*, 92.

137   "cat has a long tail" Keckley, *Behind the Scenes*, 101.

137   "sit on his stomach" Bayne, *Tad Lincoln's Father*, 48.

138   "well-meaning baboon" McPherson, *Tried by War*, 364.

139   "What shall I do?" Fehrenbacher and Fehrenbacher, *Recollected Words*, 328.

CHAPTER 8

141   "borrow it" Donald, *Lincoln*, 330.

143   "fearful smell" McClure, *Lincoln's Yarns*, 94.

143   "cross a river" Zall, *Abe Lincoln's Legacy of Laughter*, 25.

145   "the little girl...go no further" Bates, *Lincoln in the Telegraph Office*, 41.

145   "tried it on" ibid., 198.

147   "actually gone" Thomas, *Abraham Lincoln*, 303.

147   "one of the best women he ever knew" Basler, *Collected Works*, 5:326–27.

147   "day in the week" Burlingame, *Abraham Lincoln: A Life*, 1:38.

148   "more praying" Fehrenbacher and Fehrenbacher, *Recollected Words*, 362.

148   "worth looking at" Zall, *Abe Lincoln Laughing*, 142.

149   "was in the habit...without either" Fehrenbacher and Fehrenbacher, *Recollected Words*, 136.

150   "Stanton is usually right" Thomas, *Lincoln's Humor*, 12.

152   "wicked city of Chicago" Hertz, *Lincoln Talks*, 328.

153   "like shoveling fleas" ibid., 459.

154   "if it isn't good" Zall, *Abe Lincoln's Legacy of Laughter*, 64–65.

155   "hunting pet rabbits" ibid., 69.

156   "plagued few virtues" *Old Abe's Jokes*, 95.

158   "About a foot" Fehrenbacher and Fehrenbacher, *Recollected Words*, 312.

158   "How do you get out" Zall, *Abe Lincoln's Legacy of Laughter*, 97.

159   "cussing for this regiment" Fehrenbacher and Fehrenbacher, *Recollected Words*, 264.

159   "I should die" ibid., 417.

160   "be in the saddle" Gienapp, *Abraham Lincoln and Civil War America*, 113.

160   "where his hindquarters" ibid.

161   "I would save the Union" Basler, *Collected Works*, 5:388.

163   "out of his own scrape" Goodwin, *Team of Rivals*, 475.

165   "will of God prevails" Nicolay and Hay, *Complete Works of Lincoln*, 8:52–53.

166   "fatigue anything" Basler, *Collected Works*, 5:474.

166   "McClellan's bodyguard" Fehrenbacher and Fehrenbacher, *Recollected Words*, 201.

166   "at the polls" Sears, *Civil War Papers*, 493.

168   "A series of braver" Hyslop and Kagan, *Eyewitness to the Civil War*, 179.

169   "worse place than hell" McPherson, *Battle Cry of Freedom*, 574.

170   "Now I can ride" Fehrenbacher and Fehrenbacher, *Recollected Words*, 200.

170   "get into trouble" ibid., 153.

171   "God must forever bless" Basler, *Collected Works*, 5:537.

CHAPTER 9

173   "felt more certain" Fehrenbacher and Fehrenbacher, *Recollected Words*, 397.

173   "forever free" Basler, *Collected Works*, 6:29.

174   "beyond its letter" Douglass, *Life and Times*, 809.

174   "Do you know who I am..." Cooke, *Wearing of the Gray*, 118. "Mosby snickered" is author insertion.

175   "those horses cost" Zall, *Abe Lincoln Laughing*, 35.

175   "risk the dictatorship" Basler, *Collected Works*, 6:78–79.

177   "Must I shoot" ibid., 6:266.

179   "the Father of Waters" ibid., 6:409.

179   "I was wrong" ibid., 6:326.

180   "the poor devils" Dennett, *Lincoln and the Civil War*, 68.

181   "duck hit on the head" ibid., 106.

182   "not dead yet" Zall, *Abe Lincoln's Legacy of Laughter*, 30.

183   "not perish from the earth" Basler, *Collected Works*, 7:23.

184   "gets the picayune" Zall, *Abe Lincoln's Legacy of Laughter*, 66.

185   "full of old bulls" Fehrenbacher and Fehrenbacher, *Recollected Words*, 201.

185   "forty-seven pounds" Conwell, *Why Lincoln Laughed*, 4.

187   "give to everybody" Goodwin, *Team of Rivals*, 588.

187   "idea of intervention" Gienapp, *Abraham Lincoln and Civil War America*, 146.

189   "the hand of God" Burlingame, *At Lincoln's Side*, 49.

CHAPTER 10

192   "dog is always mad" Hertz, *Lincoln Talks*, 206.

193   "chin-fly biting him" McClure, *Lincoln's Yarns*, 71.

193   "darned bear go" Zall, *Abe Lincoln Laughing*, 41.

194   "your paper mill" Fehrenbacher and Fehrenbacher, *Recollected Words*, 346.

195   "little less noise" Carpenter, *Inner Life*, 49.

195   "Those not skinning" Guelzo, *Fateful Lightning*, 425.

196   "only a passenger" Fehrenbacher and Fehrenbacher, *Recollected Words*, 175.

196   "dead cavalryman" ibid., 402.

198   "to swap horses" Zall, *Abe Lincoln's Legacy of Laughter*, 19.

198   "purposes of the Almighty" Basler, *Collected Works*, 7:535.

199   "You are wrong, Speed" Speed, *Reminiscences*, 32–33.

199   "ready to be tied" ibid., 30.

200   "Atlanta is ours" Nicolay and Hay, *Complete Works of Lincoln*, 9:289.

201   "apple overboard" McClure, *Lincoln's Yarns*, 110.

202   "Calling a tail" Rice, *Reminiscences*, 62.

204   "but a noise" Carpenter, *Inner Life*, 155.

204   "legs run away" Zall, *Abe Lincoln Laughing*, 13–14.

206   "that dog, as a dog" ibid., 63.

207   "as we believe, inexhaustible" Basler, *Collected Works*, 8:151.

CHAPTER 11

211   "small 'nubbin'" Burlingame, *Abraham Lincoln: A Life*, 2:755–56.

213   "All noise" ibid., 2:756.

213   "lost his head" McPherson, *Battle Cry of Freedom*, 823.

214   "never captured" Fehrenbacher and Fehrenbacher, *Recollected Words*, 424.

215   "respectable parents" Thomas, *Lincoln's Humor*, 22.

215   "eat them immediately" Newell, *Orpheus C. Kerr Papers*, 53.

215   "footprints in the snow" Bates, *Lincoln in the Telegraph Office*, 24.

216   "became a good fox" Zall, *Abe Lincoln Laughing*, 146.

216   "shouting hullo" ibid., 109.

217   "With malice toward none" Basler, *Collected Works*, 8:332–33.

218   "my friend Douglass" Morel, *Lincoln's Sacred Effort*, 163.

218   "the Almighty and them" Basler, *Collected Works*, 8:356.

219   "make a fizzle, anyhow" Rice, *Reminiscences*, 2–4.

220   "old pair of trousers" Zall, *Abe Lincoln's Legacy of Laughter*, 69.

220   "Let 'em up easy" Thomas, *Abraham Lincoln*, 512.

221   "Lee will surrender" ibid., 513.

221   "thing be pressed" ibid.

221   "some other time" Fehrenbacher and Fehrenbacher, *Recollected Words*, 279.

221   "proposed by myself" Grant, *Personal Memoirs*, 2:495.

222   "one of the best tunes" Basler, *Collected Works*, 8:393.

222   "he will ever make" Burlingame, *Abraham Lincoln: A Life*, 2:803.

223   "frighten them out of the country" Gienapp, *Abraham Lincoln and Civil War America*, 201.

223   "enough lives had been sacrificed" ibid.

223   "some great news very soon" Welles, *Diary*, 2:282–83.

224   "Doctor...unbeknownst to meself?" Grant, *Personal Memoirs*, 2:533.

224   "Well, no...let him run" Rice, *Reminiscences*, 376.

224   "Mary later recalled...cheerfulness" Donald, *Lincoln*, 593.

224   "And well I may...very miserable." ibid.

225   "Sic Semper Tyrannis!" Guelzo, *Abraham Lincoln: Redeemer President*, 435.

226   "belongs to the ages" Donald, *Lincoln*, 599.

BIBLIOGRAPHY

Angle, Paul M. *Created Equal? The Complete Lincoln-Douglas Debates of 1858*. Chicago: University of Chicago Press, 1958.

Basler, Roy P., ed., Marion Dolores Pratt and Lloyd A. Dunlap, asst. eds. *The Collected Works of Abraham Lincoln*. New Brunswick, NJ: Rutgers University Press, 1955.

Bates, Homer. *Lincoln in the Telegraph Office: Recollections of the United States Military Telegraph Corps during the Civil War*. New York: Century, 1907.

Bayne, Julia Taft. *Tad Lincoln's Father*. New York: Little, Brown, and Company, 1931.

Bray, Robert. "What Abraham Lincoln Read—An Evaluative and Annotated List." *Journal of the Abraham Lincoln Association* 28, no. 2 (2007): 28–81.

Burlingame, Michael. *Abraham Lincoln: A Life*. Baltimore: Johns Hopkins University Press, 2008.

————, ed. *At Lincoln's Side: John Hay's Civil War Correspondence and Selected Writings*. Carbondale: Southern Illinois University Press, 2000.

————. *The Inner World of Abraham Lincoln*. Urbana: University of Illinois Press, 1994.

————. *An Oral History of Abraham Lincoln: John G. Nicolay's Interviews and Essays*. Carbondale: Southern Illinois University Press, 1996.

Carpenter, F. B. *The Inner Life of Abraham Lincoln*. Boston: Houghton, Mifflin & Co, 1883.

Conwell, Russell H. *Why Lincoln Laughed*. New York: Harper & Bros., 1922.

Cooke, John E. *Wearing of the Gray: Being Personal Portraits, Scenes, and Adventures of the War*. New York: E.B. Treat & Co., 1867.

Davis, William C. *Lincoln's Men: How President Lincoln Became a Father to an Army and a Nation*. New York: Free Press, 1999.

Dennett, Tyler. *Lincoln and the Civil War in the Diaries and Letters of John Hay*. New York: Dodd, Mead, and Company, 1939.

Dicey, Edward. "Lincolniana." *MacMillan's Magazine* 12 (June 1865): 185–92.

Dirck, Brian R. *Lincoln the Lawyer*. Urbana: University of Illinois Press, 2008.

Donald, David H. *Lincoln*. New York: Touchstone, 1996.

Douglass, Frederick. *The Life and Times of Frederick Douglass, From 1817–1882*. London: The Christian Age Office, 1882.

Duff, John J. *Abraham Lincoln, Prairie Lawyer*. New York: Rinehart and Company, 1960.

Fehrenbacher, Don E., and Virginia Fehrenbacher. *Recollected Words of Abraham Lincoln*. Stanford, CA: Stanford University Press, 1996.

Fraker, Guy C. *Lincoln's Ladder to the Presidency*. Carbondale: Southern Illinois University Press, 2012.

Frank, John P. *Lincoln as a Lawyer*. Chicago: Americana House, 1991.

Gienapp, William E. *Abraham Lincoln and Civil War America*. New York: Oxford University Press, 2002.

Goodwin, Doris Kearns. *Team of Rivals: The Political Genius of Abraham Lincoln*. New York: Simon and Schuster, 2005.

Grant, Ulysses S. *Personal Memoirs*. New York: C. L. Webster, 1885.

Guelzo, Allen C. *Abraham Lincoln: Redeemer President*. Grand Rapids, MI: William B. Eerdmans, 1999.

———. *Fateful Lightning: A New History of the Civil War and Reconstruction*. New York: Oxford University Press, 2012.

Harris, William C. *Lincoln and the Border States: Preserving the Union*. Lawrence: University Press of Kansas, 2011.

———. *Lincoln's Rise to the Presidency*. Lawrence: University Press of Kansas, 2007.

Hendrick, Burton J. *Lincoln's War Cabinet*. Boston: Little, Brown, 1946.

Herndon, William H., and Jesse K. Weik. *Herndon's Lincoln*. Chicago: Belford-Clarke Company, 1889.

Hertz, Emanuel. *The Hidden Lincoln: From the Letters and Papers of William H. Herndon.* New York: Viking Press, 1938.

———. *Lincoln Talks.* New York: Viking Press, 1939.

Hill, Frederick Trevor. *Lincoln the Lawyer.* New York: Century, 1906.

Holland, Josiah G. *Life of Abraham Lincoln.* Springfield, MA: Gurdon Bill, 1866.

Holzer, Harold. *Father Abraham: Lincoln and His Sons.* Honesdale, PA: Calkins Creek, 2011.

Hubbard, Charles M. *Lincoln Reshapes the Presidency.* Macon, GA: Mercer University Press, 2003.

Hyslop, S. G., and N. Kagan. *Eyewitness to the Civil War: The Complete History from Secession to Reconstruction.* Washington, DC: National Geographic Books, 2006.

Jaffa, Harry. *Crisis in the House Divided: An Interpretation of the Issues in the Lincoln-Douglas Debates.* Seattle: University of Washington Press, 1959.

Jones, Edgar D. *Lincoln and the Preachers.* New York: Harper & Brothers, 1948.

Jones, Howard. *The Union in Peril: The Crisis Over British Intervention in the Civil War.* Chapel Hill: University of North Carolina Press, 1992.

Keckley, Elizabeth. *Behind the Scenes, Or, Thirty Years a Slave and Four Years in the White House.* New York: G. W. Carlton, 1868.

Lamon, Dorothy, ed. *Recollections of Abraham Lincoln 1847–1865 by Ward Hill Lamon.* Chicago: A. C. McClurg and Co., 1895.

Lamon, Ward Hill. *The Life of Abraham Lincoln: From His Birth to His Inauguration as President.* Boston: James R. Osgood and Company, 1872.

McClure, Alexander K. *"Abe" Lincoln's Yarns and Stories.* Philadelphia: Winston, 1901.

McPherson, James. *Abraham Lincoln.* Oxford: Oxford University Press, 2009.

———. *Battle Cry of Freedom.* Oxford: Oxford University Press, 1988.

———. *Tried by War: Abraham Lincoln as Commander in Chief.* London: Penguin, 2008.

Miers, Earl Schenk, ed. *Lincoln Day by Day: A Chronology, 1809–1865.* Washington, DC: Lincoln Sesquicentennial Commission, 1960.

Morel, Lucas E. *Lincoln's Sacred Effort: Defining Religion's Role in American Self-Government.* Lanham, MD: Lexington Books, 2000.

Neely, Mark E. *The Abraham Lincoln Encyclopedia.* New York: Da Capo, 1982.

Newell, Robert Henry. *The Orpheus C. Kerr Papers.* New York: Blakeman and Mason, 1862.

Nicolay, John G., and John Hay, eds. *Complete Works of Lincoln.* New York: Francis D. Tandy, 1905.

Old Abe's Jokes: Fresh from Abraham's Bosom. New York: T. R. Dawley, 1864.

Phillips, Isaac N., ed. *Abraham Lincoln by Some Men Who Knew Him.* Bloomington, IL: Pantagraph Printing, 1910.

Rice, Allen T. *Reminiscences of Abraham Lincoln by Distinguished Men of His Time*. New York: North American Review, 1888.

Riddle, Donald Wayne. *Lincoln Runs for Congress*. Springfield, IL: Abraham Lincoln Association, 1948.

Scripps, John Locke. *The First Published Life of Abraham Lincoln*. 1860. Reprint, Detroit: Cranbrook Press, 1900.

Sears, Stephen W. *The Civil War Papers of George B. McClellan*. New York: Da Capo Press, 1989.

Shenk, Joshua Wolf. *Lincoln's Melancholy: How Depression Challenged a President and Fueled His Greatness*. New York: Houghton Mifflin, 2005.

Simon, Paul. *Lincoln's Preparation for Greatness: The Illinois Legislative Years*. Norman: University of Oklahoma Press, 1965.

Speed, Joshua. *Reminiscences of Abraham Lincoln and Notes of a Visit to California*. Louisville, KY: John P. Morgan and Company, 1884.

Strozier, Charles B. *Lincoln's Quest for Union: Public and Private Meanings*. New York: Basic Books, 1982.

Tarbell, Ida M., Papers. Allegheny College.

Temple, Wayne C. *Abraham Lincoln: From Skeptic to Prophet*. Mahomet, IL: Mayhaven, 1995.

Thomas, Benjamin P. *Abraham Lincoln*. New York: Alfred Knopf, 1952.

———. *"Lincoln's Humor" and Other Essays*. Edited by Michael Burlingame. Urbana: University of Illinois Press, 2002.

———. *Lincoln's New Salem*. Springfield, IL: Abraham Lincoln Association, 1934.

Trueblood, Elton. *Abraham Lincoln, Theologian of American Anguish*. New York: Harper and Row, 1973.

Walther, Eric. *William Lowndes Yancey and the Coming of the Civil War*. Chapel Hill: University of North Carolina Press, 2006.

Warren, Louis. *Lincoln's Youth: Indiana Years 1816–1830*. New York: Appleton-Century-Crofts, 1959.

Welles, Gideon. *Diary*. Edited by Howard K. Beale. New York: Norton, 1960.

White, Horace. *Abraham Lincoln in 1854*. 1908. Reprint, Charleston, SC: BiblioLife, 2009.

White, Jonathan W. *Abraham Lincoln and Treason in the Civil War: The Trials of John Merryman*. Baton Rouge: Louisiana State University Press, 2011.

Whitney, Henry. *Life on the Circuit with Lincoln*. Boston: Estes and Lauriat, 1892.

Williams, Thomas H. *Lincoln and the Generals*. New York: Alfred A. Knopf, 1952.

Wilson, Douglas, and Rodney Davis, eds. *Herndon's Informants: Letters, Interviews, and Statements about Abraham Lincoln*. Urbana: University of Illinois Press, 1998.

Wilson, Douglas L. *Honor's Voice: The Transformation of Abraham Lincoln*. New York: Alfred A. Knopf, 1998.

Wilson, Rufus Rockwell, ed. *Lincoln among His Friends: A Sheaf of Intimate Memories*. Caldwell, ID: Caxton Printers, 1942.

Wolf, William J. *The Religion of Abraham Lincoln*. New York: Seabury Press, 1963.

Woodburn, James A. *The Life of Thaddeus Stevens*. Indianapolis, IN: Bobs-Merrill, 1913.

Zall, Paul M. *Abe Lincoln Laughing*. 1982. Reprint, Knoxville: University of Tennessee Press, 1997.

———. *Abe Lincoln's Legacy of Laughter*. Knoxville: University of Tennessee Press, 2007.

PHOTO CREDITS

INDEX

Note: Illustrations are indicated by italics.

ABOUT THE AUTHOR

Gordon Leidner has been a lifelong student of Abraham Lincoln and the American Civil War. He is a member of the board of directors of the Abraham Lincoln Institute and maintains the popular history website, Great American History (www.greatamericanhistory.net). Through the website, he has provided numerous articles and free educational material about Abraham Lincoln, the American Civil War, and the American Revolution since 1996. Leidner lives near Annapolis, Maryland, with Jean, his wife of over thirty-five years.

If you have enjoyed this book, please consider *Abraham Lincoln: Quotes, Quips, and Speeches* and *The Civil War: Voices of Hope, Sacrifice, and Courage*, also by Gordon Leidner.